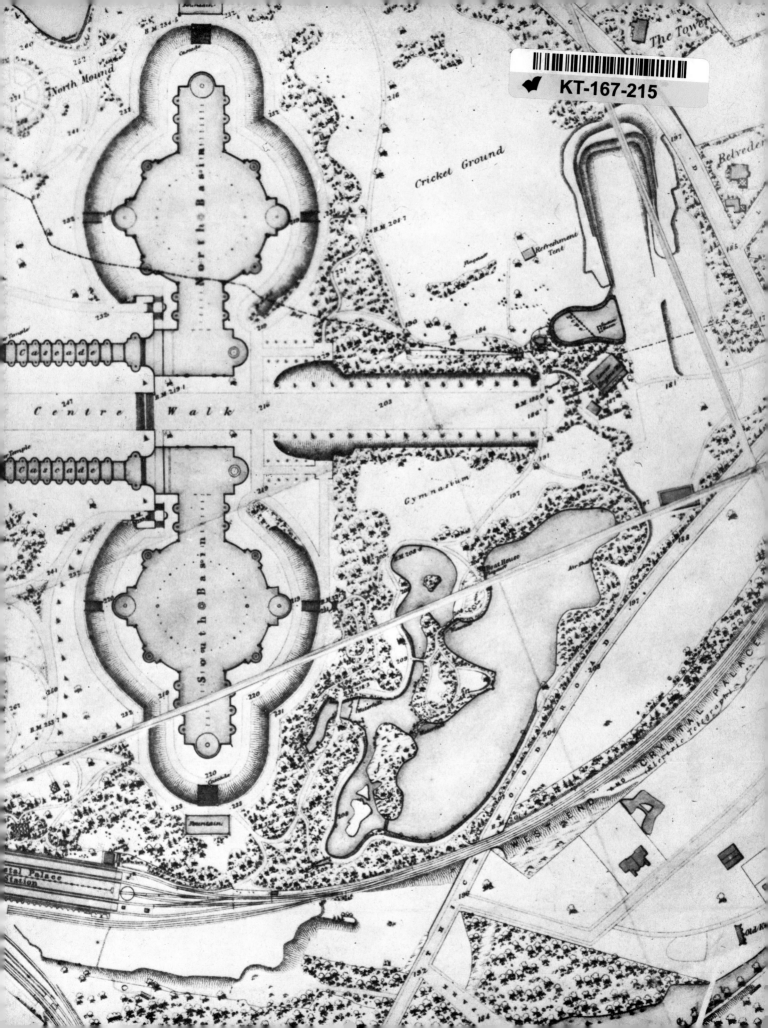

The Crystal Palace

THE CRYSTAL PALACE

1851
1936

A Portrait of Victorian Enterprise

by Patrick Beaver

HUGH EVELYN LONDON

To Amé who wishes she had seen it

by the same author The Big Ship

First published in 1970
by Hugh Evelyn Limited
9 Fitzroy Square, London W1
Reprinted 1977
© 1970, Patrick Beaver
Designed by Lawrence Edwards
Printed in Great Britain by offset lithography by
Billing & Sons Ltd, Guildford, London and Worcester
SBN 238 78961 6

CONTENTS

1
The Idea
PAGE 11

2
The Planning
PAGE 15

3
The Opposition
PAGE 21

4
The Building
PAGE 23

5
The Opening
PAGE 33

6
The Exhibits
PAGE 47

7
The Art
PAGE 57

8
The Visitors
PAGE 63

9
The Transformation
PAGE 69

10
The Winter Palace
PAGE 105

11
The End
PAGE 141

APPENDIX 1
The Hyde Park building
PAGE 150

APPENDIX 2
**Digby Wyatt's description of the
raising of the transept roof in Hyde Park**
PAGE 151

ACKNOWLEDGMENTS

The author and publishers are greatly indebted to the following individuals and institutions both for their help in collecting the illustrations and for permission to reproduce them here:
Mr Benjamin Brock
Sir Hugh Chance
Mr Douglas FitzPatrick
Mr B. E. C. Howarth-Loomes
Mr N. D. Larkin
Mr W. H. D. Lilley
Mr P. A. G. Osler
Dr D. B. Thomas
Mr and Mrs Claude Weaver of the Cambridge Tavern, Upper Norwood
The Librarian and Staff of Upper Norwood Public Library
Chance Brothers Limited
The Corcoran Gallery of Art, Washington D.C.
The Fitzroy Collection
G.L.C. Members' Library
G.L.C. Parks Department
The Guildhall Library
The Kodak Museum
The Minet Library
The Victoria and Albert Museum
John Weiss and Son Limited
In spite of strenuous efforts it has not always been possible to trace the copyright ownership of some of the illustrations, but it is hoped that any such undiscovered contributors will consider this acknowledgement as also applying to themselves. The author wishes particularly to thank his friend James Napier, who reproduced most of the photographs, often from very old and faded originals.
The author is also indebted to Miss Yvonne ffrench and the Harvill Press for permission to quote from *The Great Exhibition, 1851* and to John Murray (Publishers) Ltd for permission to quote from *1851 and the Crystal Palace* by Christopher Hobhouse.

DIMENSIONS

Hyde Park
Length of main building 1848 ft
Breadth of main building 408 ft
Height of nave 64 ft
Height of transept 108 ft
Weight of iron used 4500 tons (700 wrought, 3800 cast)
Timber 600,000 cu. ft
Panes of glass 293,655 (900,000 sq. ft)
Guttering 24 miles
Space occupied by exhibits 991,857 sq. ft
Number of exhibits over 100,000
Number of exhibitors
British 7381
Foreign 6556
TOTAL 13,937
Number of visitors
Season ticket holders 773,776
£1 days (2 days) 1042
5s days (28 days) 245,389
2s 6d days (30 days) 579,579
1s days (80 days) 4,439,419
TOTAL 6,039,205
Area of floor 772,824 sq. ft
Area of galleries 217,100 sq. ft
TOTAL 989,924 sq. ft (this figure only includes the exhibition area)

Sydenham
Length of nave 1608 ft
Width of nave 312 ft
Height of nave 68 ft
Length of each wing 574 ft
Width of transept (central) 387 ft
Height of transept 175 ft
Height of towers 284 ft
Weight of iron 9642 tons
Area of glass used 1,650,000 sq. ft superficial
Weight of glass used 500 tons
Amount of brickwork 15,391 cu. yd
Hot water piping (12 in.) 50 miles
Total area of main building 603,072 sq. ft

1

THE IDEA

'The shortest way to do many things
is to do only one thing at once'
(SAMUEL SMILES)

The Victorian Age in England, it is said, was one of optimism and, in the middle of the nineteenth century, it had good reason to be. With all her social and economic problems, England was the wealthiest and most powerful nation the world had ever known and, in spite of the appalling poverty that existed in some parts of the country and in most of the towns, the English working classes were the most prosperous in Europe. There had been no war with Europe since the defeat of Napoleon and, although the tiresome French had recently indulged in yet another blood-bath and proclaimed even yet another Republic, in 1849 the prospects looked promising for lasting peace and fellowship between all mankind – excluding, of course, the Indians, Chinese, Afghans, etc. who, because of their own naughtiness, had to be punished occasionally by the British.

When the Corn Laws were repealed in 1846 idealists cherished the hope that human energy so long occupied in the wasteful wielding of the sword would now be channelled into the peaceful rivalry of unrestricted trade between nations. One man in particular who was dedicated to this dream was Prince Albert, husband of Queen Victoria, who in 1857 was to be formally titled Prince Consort.

In 1849 Prince Albert was thirty years old and, in common with all foreigners, was distrusted and even disliked by most of the people of Britain. He had never lost his German accent and even in Court circles he was made to feel a foreigner. Yet he never ceased his exertions on behalf of his adopted country and its people. He was a serious-minded man whose only lapses into humour were through the pun and the practical joke – he once scattered a handful of stink-bombs into a theatre auditorium from the Royal Box. Baron Stockmar observed of him that in worldly and political affairs he did his best, but only from a sense of duty. Nevertheless, Albert was a man of liberal ideas, well suited to taking a leading part in the many reforms England needed at that time. His mind had a natural bent towards the artistic and he was much absorbed in the problem of improving the application of art to the manufacturing industries. Tastefulness, to Albert, was next to Godliness.

In 1847 he became President of the Society of Arts and in this capacity played a leading part in the mounting of three small exhibitions of 'Art Manufacture', in 1847, 1848 and 1849. These were promoted under the leadership of Henry Cole, an Assistant Keeper at the Record Office. At the end of the 1849 exhibition Cole approached the Prince with a most ambitious scheme for a British Exhibition of National Design and Manufacture which he proposed should be held in London in 1851. Albert agreed and, armed with the royal blessing, Cole persuaded the Department of Woods and Forests to make the courtyard of Somerset House available as a site. He then took ship for France to visit the Paris *Exposition* of 1849.

Henry Cole was one of those extraordinary Victorians who succeeded in half a dozen different careers. He had collaborated with Rowland Hill in the introduction of the Penny Post; he was editor of many journals; he was an accomplished etcher and painter and a writer of books on history, architecture and art; he was a successful music critic and writer of children's books, was instrumental in the adoption of the standard railway gauge and he published the first Christmas card. Above all he was a pioneer of industrial design, in which capacity he edited the *Journal of Design and Manufacture*.

Industrial exhibitions were the natural outcome of the Industrial Revolution. The enormous increase of manufactured goods that followed the harnessing of steam-power brought about the problems of mass marketing and the need for national shop windows. In the mid nineteenth century Britain was, indeed, the workshop of the world but it was the French themselves who deserved the reputation of being a nation of shopkeepers. They had staged the first-ever exhibition of national products as early as 1798 and, at irregular intervals, gave ten other exhibitions between then and 1849. They were all held in Paris and the last one exceeded all the others in scope and splendour.

When Cole visited the 1849 Paris *Exposition* it was not through mere curiosity. He wanted to see what the French could do so that later he could prove that the British could do better, but on seeing the size and magnificence of the French show he realized that a much larger site than the one he had in mind would be needed if the British

exhibition was to put the French to shame. Grandiose though Cole's plans were when he left for Paris, they were only for a national exhibition. When he came home his plans were larger still. France's exhibition had included the produce of her North African colonies and so why not, thought Cole, an exhibition of goods from Britain and the Empire? That would outdo the French. And why stop there? Why not ask the French themselves to exhibit in London in competition with a Britain fearless of foreign rivalry? And why not Germany, Russia – even America? In other words, why not an Exhibition of the Works of all Nations?

These were Henry Cole's thoughts when he returned to England in June 1849 and his first move was to communicate them to John Scott Russell, a fellow member of the Society of Arts. At a prize-giving of the Society later in the year, Scott Russell publicly announced that there was every hope of carrying out Prince Albert's plans for an exhibition in 1851. When this pronouncement reached the ears of the Prince he at once summoned Russell to Buckingham Palace and asked for an explanation. Russell replied that as the Commissioners of Woods and Forests had promised a site for the proposed exhibition there was nothing to prevent the Society from going ahead. At this stage nothing was said to Albert about the possibility of the exhibition being an international one and, on 27th June, Cole was summoned in turn by the Prince to discuss the project.

Albert's purpose in meeting Cole was to discuss the Somerset House site and the building that would house the exhibition, but Cole used the audience as an opportunity to expound his great idea. For centuries Europe had worshipped the sword. Here was an opportunity to exalt the creative rather than the destructive, through the presentation of the quiet industry of the craftsman. Why not, therefore, hold an international rather than a national exhibition? This was

Owen Jones.

Hyde Park in the mid nineteenth century.

Matthew Digby Wyatt.

music to the Prince's ears but it took him a minute or so to grasp the implications of so novel an idea. He hesitated and then finally decided. 'It must', he said to Cole, 'embrace foreign productions . . . it *must* be international.'

Cole pressed his opportunity. The Somerset House site, he said, would be totally inadequate to accommodate an exhibition of such scope. Other sites were proposed, discussed and rejected, then Cole suggested Hyde Park. The Prince thought this might be a good idea and instructed Cole to examine the Park and report on a suitable site. Cole lost no time – there was none to spare. Never before had such an exhibition been held and 1851 was a mere eighteen months ahead. A site had to be found, legislation obtained, money raised. Then a building would have to be designed and built capable of housing and showing off the products of the entire civilized world. That same afternoon Cole went to the Park and chose a suitable site opposite Knightsbridge Barracks. By the following day his report was ready and he presented it to the Prince who gave it his assent.

In that Golden Age of *laissez-faire* it did not even occur to Cole to seek financial backing for the scheme from the Government. If there were to be an exhibition it would, as a matter of course, have to be self-supporting; the first task was to raise

the estimated £100,000 that would be required. A Mr Fuller offered to put up £20,000 for prizes and through the agency of the same gentleman a firm of contractors, Messrs James and George Munday, offered to finance the entire scheme in exchange for two-thirds of the total receipts. Prince Albert accepted this offer, but with reservations, feeling that a scheme for the promotion of peace and goodwill should not be based on outright commercial speculation, so a proviso was inserted into Messrs Mundays' contract that required them to withdraw if the money could be raised by private and public subscription. In the event Mundays' were forced to withdraw and missed profits that would have amounted to some £170,000.

A Royal Commission was formed early in 1850 with the Prince as its President. Its members included Lord Russell (the Prime Minister), Peel, Gladstone, Cobden, William Cubitt and Charles Barry, the architect. The Commission's first decision was to raise the required money through public subscription; it revoked Mundays' contract and paid them an agreed sum of £5120 in compensation. Under the Royal Commission an Executive Committee was formed with Robert Stephenson as Chairman and the architect and art critic Matthew Digby Wyatt as Secretary. Wyatt was a member of a family that proliferated in artists and architects and he was famous for his catholic knowledge and use of architectural styles. In 1849 he had been employed by the Society of Arts to write a report on the Paris *Exposition* and it was the ableness and comprehensiveness of this report that led the Commissioners to engage him as secretary to the Executive Committee. The first action of the Committee was to invite subscriptions and, after a slow start, the money poured in. Meetings and Mansion House banquets produced over £10,000 and in a little over a year £79,224 had been subscribed with a further £250,000 underwritten by manufacturers and businessmen. Collecting-boxes were circulated in the working-class areas so that even the labourer could subscribe his penny towards a project that would, it was thought, better his lot by promoting trade, understanding and peace between the nations of the world.

The flow of money was accompanied by a flow of applications for floor-space and by the beginning of 1850 the demand for space by British exhibitors alone amounted to some 500,000 square feet. Evidently the 1851 Exhibition was going to be the biggest show the world had ever seen. At least a million square feet would be required and it had not yet been decided how it was to be housed. In January a Building Committee was formed consisting of the Duke of Buccleuch, Lord Ellesmere, Cubitt, Donaldson – Professor of Architecture at London University, Robert Cockerell – then engaged in building St George's Hall in Liverpool, Barry (who had built the new Houses of Parliament) and the two giants of engineering, Robert Stephenson and I. K. Brunel. The final site had been fixed as stretching between Rotten Row and Kensington Gate and the world's architects were invited to submit designs for the Exhibition building in free competition. 'Two hundred and forty-five plans were submitted as a result by all sorts and conditions of men, from Mr Crace, the fashionable decorator of Wigmore Street, down to "Sed quis custodiet custodes" and Lady (A) with great diffidence submits this plan.'*

After examining all the plans put forward, the Committee made the surprising announcement that they could not recommend the adoption of any of them and had therefore prepared a plan of their own, tenders for which would be invited in due course.

Meanwhile, building or no building, the Foreign Secretary was busy communicating with every manufacturing country in the world asking them to participate.

* Christopher Hobhouse, *1851 and the Crystal Palace*, John Murray, 1937, p. 16.

'The Royal Commissioners for the Exhibition of 1851.'
From the painting in the Victoria and Albert Museum, London, by H. W. Phillips. The commissioners are, left to right; Standing: C. W. Dilke, John Scott Russell, Henry Cole, Charles Fox, Joseph Paxton, Lord John Russell, Sir Robert Peel, Robert Stephenson; Seated: Richard Cobden, Charles Barry, Lord Grenville, William Cubitt, Prince Albert, Lord Derby.

2

THE PLANNING

'. . . a greenhouse larger than ever
greenhouse was built before'
(JOHN RUSKIN)

The Building Committee's design for an exhibition building is a prime example of what results when creative work is undertaken by a Committee instead of an artist. The fact that the Committee included among its members three distinguished architects and two of history's greatest engineers may help to account for the reason why their brainchild was so misbegotten; moreover it is safe to assume that they ransacked the 245 submitted designs for ideas. This would account for the hideous hybridity of their design.

The proposed building, which was four times as long as St Paul's Cathedral, resembled a huge railway station. The entrance was flanked by false arches of enormous misproportions and on the end of this dreary edifice there squatted an iron dome, 200 feet wide and 150 feet high. The dome was Brunel's creation and was the worst thing he ever did.

This, then, was the design that the Committee proudly presented. The public reaction to it was so violent and derisory that for a time the whole scheme for an exhibition was in jeopardy. Early murmurings of dissent had been heard in March when Lord Brougham expressed in the House of Lords his fears that Britain was about to make an 'exhibition' of herself; but in rejecting all the submitted designs the Committee had made

an irrevocable decision – its own much-cherished design was a laughing-stock and yet, if the building was not started within a few days, it could not be finished in time. But what alternative was there?

In June 1850, with less than a year to go before the opening date of the Exhibition, Mr Joseph Paxton was taken by his friend, Mr John Ellis, MP, to visit Henry Cole at the Board of Trade. Paxton was, among other things, a self-taught architect who specialized in building with glass and iron. He had heard of the difficulties concerning the Exhibition building and thought he might be able to help. Paxton was a remarkable man, even for an age that abounded in remarkable men. As the self-made man who started his working life without even the advantage of an elementary education he seems to step from the pages of *Self-Help* and it is curious that Smiles does not include him among the examples he gives of that inestimable virtue. The son of a farmer, he was born in 1801 in the village of Milton Bryant in Bedfordshire and at twenty-one he was employed as under-gardener in the arboretum of the Horticultural Society's gardens at Chiswick. Here his work came to the notice of the Duke of Devonshire, himself a keen horti-culturist, and Paxton at the age of twenty-three was offered the post of head

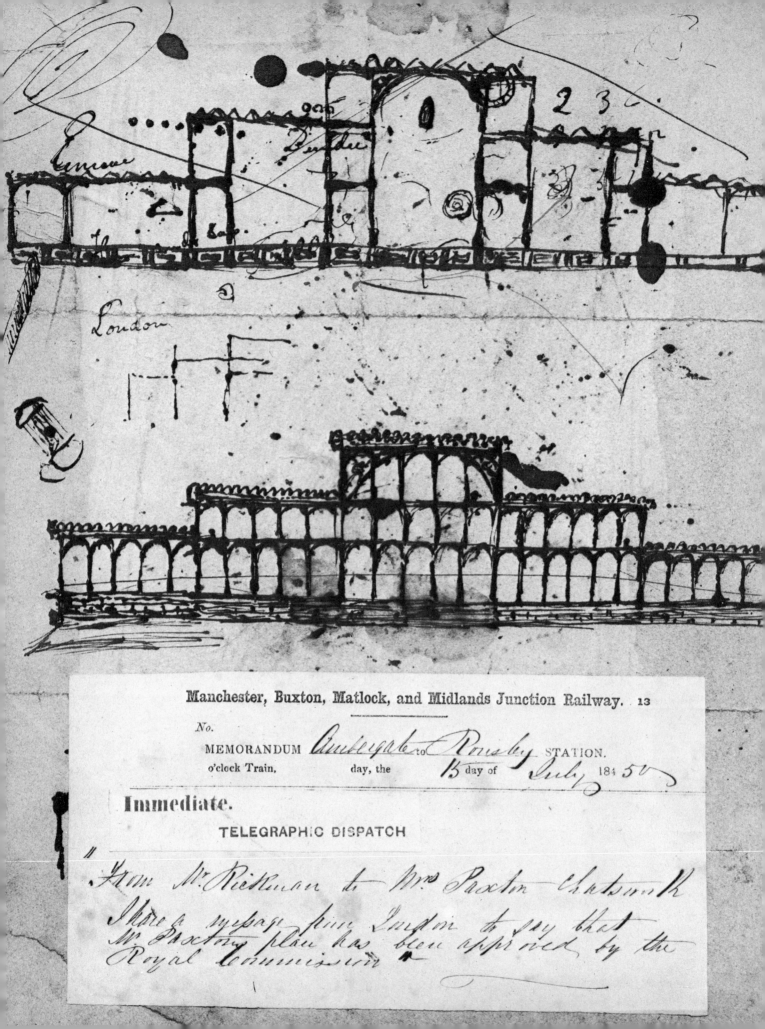

Manchester, Buxton, Matlock, and Midlands Junction Railway. 13

No.

MEMORANDUM *Ambergate* to *Rowsley* STATION.

o'clock Train,   day, the   15 day of   *July*   184 5b

Immediate.

TELEGRAPHIC DISPATCH

From Mr Rickman to Mrs Paxton Chatsworth I have a message from London to say that Mr Paxton's plan has been approved by the Royal Commission

Paxton's original sketch for a glass
exhibition building. It was executed within
a few minutes at a railway board meeting.
Apart from the lack of a transept it
resembles almost exactly the building that
was put up in Hyde Park. Below is the
telegram accepting the design.

gardener on the Duke's estate at Chatsworth. By the time he was forty, Paxton
had become the Duke's 'admirable
Crichton' and friend and when he met
Cole he was already a very wealthy man.
He was manager of Devonshire's estates
at Chatsworth, Chiswick, Devonshire
House, Bolton Abbey, Hardwick and
Lismore. He had made a fortune from
the railways as both a director and an
investor. In addition he had built bridges,
reservoirs and gasworks. He designed
and built the model village of Edensor
and at Chatsworth he built fountains,
orchid houses and an aboretum. His
masterpiece was the Great Conservatory
at Chatsworth which covered an acre of
ground. In his spare time he started the
Daily News under the editorship of
Charles Dickens.

In 1837 a British traveller in Guiana
discovered a huge, beautiful water-lily,
some seeds of which he brought back to
England and presented to Kew Gardens.
Here they were tended with the greatest
care but although they germinated they
never grew to any size and they would not
flower. Paxton obtained a cutting of the
plant and put it into a heated tank at
Chatsworth. Still the lily did not prosper
so Paxton designed paddle-wheels to
keep the water moving. The plant then
behaved like Jack's beanstalk and in
three months it had reached enormous
proportions. There were eleven leaves,
each 5 feet in diameter, and huge beautiful blooms. Paxton named his lily Victoria
Regia and presented the Queen with a
bud.

Still the lily grew and Paxton was
faced with the necessity of building a
special house for it. One day, to test the
buoyancy of the leaves, he placed his
little daughter on one of them and noticed
that it took her weight without the least
distortion. He then studied the underside
of the leaf – the radiating ribs strengthened
by cross-ribs – and decided to use the
Victoria Regia as a pattern for the lily-
house. The result was a light airy structure with a glass roof supported by light
wooden beams which were hollowed out

into gutters. These beams were supported
in turn by light tubular columns of iron
which also acted as drains for the roof.
The result was charming and most
economical to build.

The lily-house had not long been built
when Paxton made the visit to his friend
Ellis at the new House of Commons. The
acoustics of Barry's building, having
proved unsatisfactory, were at the time
undergoing a series of tests. Paxton observed that mistakes had, indeed, been
made in the building: 'I was afraid that
they would also commit a blunder in the
building for the Industrial Exhibition;
I told him [Mr Ellis] I had a notion in
my head and that I would ascertain
whether it was too late to send in a design.'[*]
Ellis was aware that the heavy misgivings
concerning the proposed brick and iron
structure were now shared by the Building Committee itself and he at once took
his friend to the Board of Trade to
introduce him to Henry Cole. From Cole
Paxton learned that the Committee was
prepared to consider another proposal
providing it was submitted, complete
with detailed drawings, within two weeks.
'Then I will go home and in nine days
time I will bring you my plans all complete', said Paxton. Years later he re-
called: 'The Committee thought me a
conceited fellow and that what I said was
nearer romance than common sense.'

From the Board of Trade, Paxton
walked to the Hyde Park site and in-
spected the ground. By the time he
reached his London home his mind was
made up. He would design a building of
glass and iron – a vastly magnified version
of the lily-house at Chatsworth. Being
light and airy, such a building would be
ideally suitable for an exhibition. It
would be cheap, simple to put up and,
containing no bricks and mortar, would
be dry and ready for immediate use. Also
(and this would answer a large body of
anti-Exhibition agitation) it could be
taken down later, leaving the Park un-
scarred, and if necessary it could be
rebuilt elsewhere. At the worst the glass
and iron would have a high scrap value.

* Paxton, *Illustrated London News*, vol. 17,
p. 322.

All the objections to the Committee's plan were met by Paxton's simple but ingenious idea.

Paxton had nine days in which to design in detail a building with a capacity of some 33,000,000 cubic feet. The first two of these days were taken up with watching the floating and raising of the third tube of Robert Stephenson's Britannia Bridge which still spans the Menai Straits; during these two days, however, his mind must have been constantly at work on his great idea for on the third day, at a Midland Railway meeting, Paxton put pen to paper and within a few minutes produced a sketch of a ferro-vitreous building almost identical to the one eventually built in Hyde Park. When the railway meeting came to an end, Paxton fairly flew back to his office in Chatsworth and there, within a week and with the help of only his usual assistants, he drew up detailed plans for a building 1848 feet long and 450 feet wide. The speed with which he finished the task is even more amazing when it is considered that he was designing a structure in glass for which there were no established building methods. The heavy duty on glass had been lifted only six years previously, and before that only the rich like Paxton's employer could afford to use it on a large scale. '. . . Glass was no more regarded in 1850 as a building material than alabaster is today.'*

The building had to be capable of accommodating tens of thousands of visitors at one time and displaying the arts and manufactures of the whole world but at the same time it also had to be a purely temporary structure. In the event, Paxton's Crystal Palace withstood the hail, storm and other ravages of time for eighty-five years and was structurally as sound in 1936 as it was in 1851.

* Hobhouse, op. cit., p. 32.

**St Paul's Cathedral out of Euston Station!
The design for an exhibition building
submitted by the Building Committee.**

After some passing resistance from the Building Committee, who were apprehensive of such a revolutionary approach, the design was accepted providing that it could be constructed at a lower cost than that of the Committee's bantling. Paxton was given one week to submit the tender. He at once contacted Messrs Fox and Henderson, a firm of building contractors in Smethwick, and Messrs Chance Brothers of Birmingham, who were the only glass manufacturers in England capable of producing the enormous quantities of glass that the building would require. Within a week the working drawings and quantity estimates had been prepared, down to the nearest pound of iron and pane of glass. Charles Dickens wrote in *Household Words*:

'There is no one circumstance in the history of manufacturing enterprise of the English nation which places in so strong a light as this its boundless resources in materials, to say nothing of the marvellous arithmetical skill in compiling at what cost and in how short a time they can be converted to a special purpose. What was done in those few days? Two parties in London, relying on the accuracy and good-will of a single ironmaster, the owners of a single glass-works in Birmingham, and of one master-carpenter in London, bound themselves for a certain sum of money and in the course of some months to cover eighteen acres of ground with a building upwards of a third of a mile long . . .'

Oil-lamps must have burned through the nights of that short week in the offices of Fox and Henderson and their subcontractors, for the drawings and estimates produced would normally have taken months. The building called for huge quantities of standardized, prefabricated parts and any error in the quantity surveying might have been multiplied hundreds of times. Paxton's plans demanded 205 miles of sash-bars, 3300 iron columns and 2150 girders as well as some 900,000 square feet of glass comprising 293,655 panes, and 600,000 cubic feet of timber.

The figure arrived at was £150,000, which worked out at almost a penny per cubic foot of building, but Fox and Henderson offered to build the whole thing for £79,800 if, when the Exhibition was over, they could keep the materials. Even the larger figure was well below the estimated cost of putting up the iron and brick monstrosity that the Committee had envisaged. It had no option but to accept the tender of £79,800 and to authorize Fox and Henderson to proceed at full speed. The architect Owen Jones* was appointed as Superintendent of Works.

The Committee wanted one alteration to Paxton's design. It had occurred to themselves that if the building was to be an enormous glasshouse, there would be no need to continue with the work of clearing the trees from the site. The murmurs of opposition to the whole idea of the Exhibition had crescendoed alarmingly when it was announced that some elms in the Park would have to be removed to make way for the building. In those quieter days a tree was not considered a mere excrescence which, if it stood in the way of road-building or other development, had to be removed. Squares and parks were jealously guarded by town-dwellers who did not, as we do, take for granted the juggernaut of urban development. Some elm trees had already been uprooted from the Park and the popular reaction to this had been strong enough to threaten the very idea of the Exhibition – or at any rate, its siting in London.

The Building Committee saw Paxton's great glass hall as a straw that could be clutched at so they asked Fox and Henderson if they would include in their price the construction of an arched transept in the centre of the building large enough to cover the threatened elms. This was agreed and the contractors occupied the site on 30th July. The problem of the elms therefore gave rise, almost gratuitously, to Paxton's graceful transept which gave the building its distinguished appearance.

* Owen Jones (1809–74) was the only son of a celebrated antiquary of the same name. His forte was interior decoration.

Colonel Charles de Laet Waldo Sibthorpe, MP for Lincoln. His father, Colonel Waldo Sibthorpe, had been MP for Lincoln and his son Waldo Sibthorpe was also MP for Lincoln. Both his brother and his great-uncle had been MPs for Lincoln.*

3

THE OPPOSITION

'Woodman, spare that tree'
(GEORGE POPE MORRIS)

The first sign of the storm to come was a rumble of distant thunder from *The Times* in 1849. Commenting on a banquet given in Paris to the Lord Mayor and Corporation of the City of London to celebrate the idea of the Exhibition the *Times* leader asked, 'What do the Lord Mayor and Corporation of London represent but jobbery and good living, not to say gluttony and corruption?' Before long the Great Exhibition became one of the main topics of letters to the Editor of *The Times*; doctors warned that the expected influx of foreign visitors would bring with it an epidemic of the plague while others saw in the threatened invasion a spreading of venereal disease throughout Britain. Clergymen wrote that the scheme was arrogant and, in flying in the face of God, was likely to call forth his wrath. The main and most virulent objectors were manufacturers who feared ruin if England were flooded with cheap foreign goods. By June 1850 *The Times* had worked itself into a state of blind panic and was warning its readers that 'The whole of Hyde Park and . . . the whole of Kensington Gardens, will be turned into a bivouac of all the vagabonds of London . . .' and a little later it reported that foreigners were renting houses near Hyde Park to be used as brothels.

To the head of this army of dissent sprang a most able champion, Colonel Charles de Laet Waldo Sibthorpe, ultra-tory, ultra-protestant MP for Lincoln. A man of eccentric dress and manner he had successfully opposed the granting of £50,000 a year to Prince Albert because he, the Colonel, did not like foreigners. He was against Catholic Emancipation through his private dislike of Catholicism and had always opposed Railway Bills because he, personally, opposed railways. He was a sturdy adversary of Parliamentary reform and free trade and early in 1850 he had fought the Public Libraries Act because, as he said in the House, he did not much care for reading at all. As an antagonist of free trade the very idea of an international Exhibition had brought him near to apoplexy but not until the matter of the trees came before the Commons was the Colonel able to find an effective platform. On 18th June 1850 he asked the House: 'Are the elms to be sacrificed for one of the greatest frauds, greatest humbugs, greatest absurdities ever known?'; then, in the same speech and shifting cleverly to another target, 'I will· do nothing to encourage foreigners – nothing to give secret service money to them in the shape of premiums paid to strangers . . .', and then, for good measure, '. . . they are going to expend £26,000 [*sic*] on this building when the Irish poor are starving'.

By 4th July Sibthorpe was well into

* Writers on the Great Exhibition spell the Colonel's name both with and without the final 'e'. The present writer selected Sibthorpe but on going to press discovered that he had chosen wrongly.

the stride that he was to maintain for the next three years – '. . . the trees in Hyde Park have been cut down at the mere caprice of the Commissioners of Woods and Forests. . . . A gentleman who lives near Hyde Park and who pays £110 ground rent for his home told me that he was admiring the trees one evening before going to bed, and when he got up in the morning to shave, they were gone! The gentleman thought that some thieves had run away with them, for it did not occur to him to suspect the Commissioners of Woods and Forests.' And then, 'the object of the promoters is to introduce amongst us foreign stuff of every description, without regard to quality or quantity . . . [and to] pave the way for the establishment of cheap and nasty trash and trumpery. . . . It would be better for the promoters of this affair to encourage native industry, and support the industrious people of England, from whom they draw all they possess.' '"Live and let live" is my maxim' was the paradoxical ending of this speech. Eight days later Sibthorpe learned that the remaining trees on the site had been saved by Paxton's great transept and his most effective weapon was gone. Outflanked but undaunted, he returned to the attack with a new one: 'It is becoming the general impression in this country that there has never been a greater humbug, a greater fraud, a greater injustice than this proposed exhibition. . . . Who will pay [for it]. . . ? The foreigner? Why, he has no money. . . . The House has been told that labourers throughout the country will save their shillings, that they might be enabled to visit the exhibition. Who will take care of their families whilst they are away in London? The poor labourers are to come up to London, helter-skelter, where they will suddenly find themselves amidst the temptations of the great metropolis. . . . What will become of the chastity and the modesty of those who might become unsuspecting victims of those temptations?'

On the very day when Fox and Henderson were given their contract the Colonel reached a pitch of near hysteria that was probably brought on by despair. He called the Exhibition '. . . a purpose prejudicial to the people in a moral, religious and social point of view. . . . An exhibition of the industry of all nations, forsooth! An exhibition of the trumpery and trash of foreign countries! . . . The promoters of the project are flying in the face of the rights of the public merely to gratify the foreigner, who has no right to be here at all.'

Finally, Sibthorpe asked the Attorney-General whether it was true that he had refused his sanction to an application to the Court of Chancery for an injunction to stay the holding of the exhibition in Hyde Park. The Attorney-General replied that he had!

Within eight weeks the site had been cleared and the first upright columns were in place.

4

THE BUILDING

'I, who late sung Belgravia's charms,
Now sing the Crystal Palace'
(MRS GASCOYNE)

Messrs Fox and Henderson took possession of the site on 30th July 1850 and they undertook to complete the building by the last day of the same year. Thus they had just five months in which to complete a building that would cover 19 acres of ground and enclose 33,000,000 cubic feet.* The area of the ground floor was to be 772,824 square feet and that of the galleries 217,100 square feet. The nave was to be 64 feet high and the central transept 408 feet long and 108 feet high.

The first eight weeks were spent in levelling the ground and laying the concrete foundations together with the iron pipes which were to serve the double purpose of holding the iron columns and draining the water that would run through the columns from the roof. The total length of the pipes was over 34 miles. Then, on 26th September, the first upright columns were raised. To elevate these a pair of shear-legs was used. This consisted simply of two poles lashed together at the top and held in position by ropes which extended from the apex of the triangle formed by the poles and the base-line of the ground to stakes driven into the ground some distance away. Ropes were passed through pulleys attached to the apex and, by their means, the columns and cross-ribbed girders were hoisted into place. Connecting

pieces were fixed to the head of each column and as soon as two columns were fixed in place a girder was hoisted and secured between the connecting pieces. An opposite pair of columns with their girder was then erected and two more girders made up the square. The shoring pieces, together with the shear-legs, were then moved on and the operation was repeated.

When the building of the first storey was under way a second team of workmen followed erecting the next. This was effected with a longer pair of shear-legs and, in the same way, the third tier was secured. Thus the iron framework of the whole building was erected without the use of scaffolding. Meanwhile, miles of 'Paxton guttering'* were being manufactured on the site by special machinery, and steam-engines were drilling, punching and cutting the wrought-iron trusses that were to span the central nave.

The speed with which the work was done is amazing. Paxton himself reported seeing the erection of three columns and two girders within sixteen minutes. As the great iron structure grew, more men were taken on until, by the end of the year, the original work force of 39 men had grown into one of over 2000.

In October work was started on the formation of the transept ribs. Their shape was first set out on a platform built

---

* Although the main structure was finished on time the building was not finally completed until the end of March.

* See Appendix 1.

23

for the purpose, and the timbers for the first rib were laid on it and shaped. When this rib was completed it was used as a template for the second; this process continued until the sixteen transept ribs had been completed. The raising of the ribs was started on 4th December and within a week they were all in place. No sooner had the skeleton of the transept roof been completed than the work of glazing was begun. Much of this was effected with the aid of special trolleys, the wheels of which ran along the grooves in Paxton's guttering. By means of this simple machine, eighty men, in the space of one week, fixed more than 18,000 panes of glass – at least 62,600 square feet super-

ficial. One man fixed no less than 108 panes during one day. At one point these glaziers went on strike for a rise from four shillings to five shillings per day. This was swiftly and effectively dealt with for Messrs Fox and Henderson could afford neither delay nor blackmail. The ringleaders were dismissed and the rest given the chance to go back to work at the old agreed rate. They went back to the job which entailed laying 900,000 square feet of glass. As the glaziers moved across the roof they were followed on the inside of the building by nearly 500 painters who worked along a veritable maze of scaffolding. The inside of the hall was decorated in red, white, blue and

Left Raising the trusses of the nave.

Top right Erecting the first columns.

Right The elm in the south-west part of the building.

Extreme right Raising a pair of the transept ribs (see Appendix 2).

CONTINUED ON PAGE 28

eft General view of the works.

ottom left Moving a pair of transept ribs amed together prior to hoisting.

elow Top of a column with a connecting ece.

Top Glazing the roof.

Centre Paxton's glazing wagons. These could be covered as a protection from the rain.

Bottom Metal punching machine.

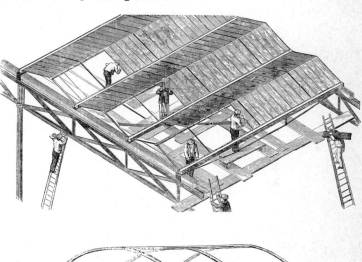

yellow and the outside in stone picked out in light blue. No sooner was the paint dry than another army of workmen, this time the joiners, followed through the building and constructed the 11 miles of stalls that were to display the 100,000 exhibits already beginning to arrive at Hyde Park from all over the world.

On 4th February the Speech from the Throne referred to the healthy state of trade and manufacture and during the following debate the indefatigable Member for Lincoln rallied his powers of oratory in an effort, even at this late stage, to damn the Commission and its work: 'that fraud upon the public called a "Glass House"... that accursed building, erected to encourage the foreigner at the expense of the already grievously-distressed English artisan. Would to God – I have often wished it – that a heavy hailstorm or a visitation of lightning would put a stop to the further progress of that work. Your property, your wives and families will be at the mercy of pickpockets and whoremongers from every part of the earth.' But by now Paxton's beautiful structure, soaring and glittering above the park, had captured the heart of the whole nation – rich and poor alike. *Punch*, originally sceptical of the whole scheme, had already dubbed the building 'Crystal Palace' (invoking from the indomitable Colonel the lone and distant rumble: 'Crystal Palace, forsooth – Palace of Tomfoolery') and William Thackeray was moved to write:

'But yesterday a naked sod
    The dandies sneered from Rotten Row
And cantered o'er it to and fro:
    And see 'tis done!

'As though 'twere by a wizard's rod
    A blazing arch of lucid glass
Leaps like a fountain from the grass
    To meet the sun!'

The opening of the 'Great Exhibition of the Works of Industry of all Nations', as it was now officially called, was fixed for 1st May and well before that date the building, its interior decoration, stalls, exhibits and amenities were ready. From the cutting of the first sod the whole tremendous enterprise had been completed in less than nine months. Apart from the little strike there had been no incidents to slow down the work. Such luck could not last. A crisis was to hand and it descended in April, only two weeks before the expected opening. Escaping from the March cold of Hyde Park, a number of sparrows had found their way into the building before the roof had been completed. They not only nested in the elms but spent the day flying round the nave and perching on the trusses and girders. Victorian sparrows they might have been but they had no inhibitions concerning their natural functions. The appearance, as well as the value, of the world's art and manufacture was not enhanced by being exposed in what was rapidly becoming, through the propagation of the feathered lodgers, a vast aviary. Poison had failed and guns, owing to the prohibition that applies to people living in glass houses, were obviously out of the question. Paxton, Stephenson – even the great Brunel – applied their minds to the problem in vain. What was to be done? News of the deadlock was brought to the Queen herself. She knew the answer. 'Send for the Duke,' she said. Wellington came and learned the details of the dilemma with the calm that had immortalized his name on the field of Waterloo. The Queen and her Court waited as the Iron Duke weighed the problem in his mind. Then he spoke. 'Try sparrow-hawks, Ma'am.' He had won his final victory.

Right and below left Sash-bar grooving machine.

Below right Gutter cutting machine.

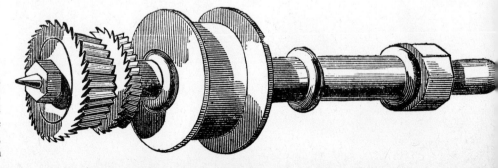

The completed building in Hyde Park. This picture is the most informative of the hundreds produced at the time. The iron and glass boiler house is in the lower right-hand corner.

5
THE OPENING

'Foreigners also came, their bearded faces conjuring
up all the horrors of Free Trade'

(The Times)

From the beginning of the year until the day of opening there were never less than 2000 men employed in putting the finishing touches to the huge yet elegant building that gleamed in the sun of a fortunately mild winter. From the middle of February onwards the activity and the number of people around the Palace steadily increased as the exhibits arrived from all over the world. There were 14,000 exhibitors – half of them British – and the stream of incoming goods gradually grew into an avalanche. Along with the consumer goods, samples of raw materials and works of art came huge pieces of industrial machinery, agricultural implements, great monoliths and blocks of coal, carriages, wagons and locomotives – all delivered by teams of horses. It was a superb piece of organization: within the space of three months over 100,000 articles were received at the site and each one channelled to its correct place on the 11 miles of stalls. One parcel arrived from France addressed to 'Sir Vyatt and Sir Fox Enderson Esquire, Grate Exposition Park of Hide at London. GLACE SOFTLY TO BE POSED UPRIGHT.'

With the goods came the vanguard of the foreign and colonial exhibitors with their staffs, and on seeing the actual presence in London of the foreigners ne so hated and dreaded, Colonel Sibthorpe seemed to take leave of his senses. 'That miserable Crystal Palace,' he roared in anguish, 'that wretched place where every species of fraud and immorality will be practised. Let them [the Commissioners] beware of man-traps and spring guns. They will have their food robbed – they will have a piebald generation, half black and half white; but I can assure them that my arm will be raised to prevent such a violation. They might look for assassinations, for being stabbed in the dark; but careless of that, I am determined to pursue an even, straightforward course, and I would say that my dearest wish is that that confounded building called the Crystal Palace might be dashed to pieces.' But by this time the Hon. Member for Lincoln was crying alone in

a wilderness. The whole nation was Exhibition mad. Even *The Times* was purring although it grumbled a little about the lack of 'conveniences for foreigners, who are not particular when certain calls of nature press, where they stop to relieve themselves'.

Meanwhile, 25,000 season tickets had been sold at three guineas for gentlemen and two guineas for ladies. The holders of these tickets had the privilege of attending on the day when the Great Exhibition was opened by the Queen. For the two days following the opening the price of admission was to be one pound and thereafter five shillings until 24th May. Then it was to be reduced to one shilling from Mondays to Thursdays, half a crown on Fridays and five shillings on Saturdays. There would be no Sunday opening. Smoking, alcohol and dogs were prohibited.

By the end of April, London was packed with visitors. Hotels and boarding-houses were continually full and many visitors had to take accommodation up to 20 miles out of the capital. Notices claiming proficiency in all the European languages appeared in shop windows and the *Morning Chronicle* was printing articles in English, German and French in parallel columns.

So great was the demand for cabs that every available vehicle capable of such use was pressed into service. Hundreds of ancient and decrepit carriages helped to create a London traffic problem that was to last for nearly six months. To add to the crush, the capital was garrisoned with soldiers to deal with possible disturbances. A company of artillery was stationed in the Tower, while five cavalry regiments (two of which were of lancers), and seven battalions of infantry protected the Park itself. In addition 6000 extra police were on duty in London.

The morning of 1st May was a bright and genial one and before eleven o'clock there were 500,000 people in the Park. Charles Spencer, the great aeronaut, was there in his balloon waiting to ascend at the moment when the Exhibition was

Left The west end of the building.

Below left The north-west corner of the building.

Below The east end of the building.

Following pages: left Inside the transept showing Sibthorpe's elms, Osler's Crystal Fountain and part of the Coalbrookdale iron gates. The interior photographs of the Great Exhibition were taken by Fox Talbot on Sundays when the Exhibition was closed.

Right Osler's Crystal Fountain: 27 feet high, it was made from 4 tons of pure crystal glass.

I can understand people not turning up I wouldn't

declared open. On the Serpentine was a model frigate, fully manned and ready to fire a salute on the Queen's arrival. There was great apprehension about firing guns in the vicinity of a glass building, for *The Times* had warned that the 'concussion will shiver the glass roof of the Palace, and thousands of ladies will be cut into mincemeat'.

By midday over 1000 carriages of state had arrived at the Park gates together with 1500 cabs, 800 broughams, 600 post carriages, 300 clarences and 300 other vehicles. The jam stretched from the Park gates to the Strand. Promptly at twelve o'clock the Queen and Prince Albert arrived and were greeted by the salute of the guns. There must have been sighs of relief in the Crystal Palace when the ladies were found to be unscathed.

Beneath the great glass roof, upwards of 30,000 people were awaiting the Queen's entry and the scene was described by one of the spectators: 'The shock of delighted surprise which everyone felt on first entering the great transept of Joseph Paxton's building was a sensation as noble as it was deep. Its vastness was measured by the huge elms, two of the giants of the park, which rose far into the air with all their wealth of foliage as free and unconfined as if there was nothing between them and the open sky. The plash of fountains, the luxuriance of tropical foliage, the play of colours from the choicest flowers, carried on into the vistas of the nave by the rich dyes of carpets and stuffs from the costliest looms, were enough to fill the eye and mind with a pleasure never to be forgotten, even without the vague sense of what lay beyond in the accumulated results of human ingenuity and cultivated art. One general effect of beauty has been produced by the infinitely varied work of the thousands who had separately co-operated towards this marvellous display; and the structure in which it was set, by its graceful lines and the free play of light which is admitted, seemed to fulfil

37

every condition that could be desired for setting off the treasures thus brought together.'*

On entering the transept the Queen took her place on the dais, surrounded by her ladies-in-waiting and some of the most illustrious statesmen and warriors of the age. The great organ sounded the National Anthem and it was taken up by 'a multitude of voices, like the sound of mighty waters'. Prince Albert then descended from the dais and read the report of the Commission to which the Queen made a brief reply. The Archbishop of Canterbury offered a short prayer which was followed by the 'Hallelujah Chorus'. Then a procession, with the Royal Family at its head, walked through the entire length of the building. On the return to the dais there was a fanfare of trumpets and the Exhibition was declared open.

Throughout the whole proceedings there had not been the slightest incident to mar the delight of the occasion. Lord Palmerston wrote later, 'It was impossible for the invited guests of a lady's drawing room to have conducted themselves with more perfect propriety than did this sea of human beings.'

The Queen recorded her impressions in her journal:

'The glimpse of the transept through the iron gates, the waving palms, flowers,

* Rev. James Taylor, DD, *The Age We Live In*, William Mackenzie, 1888.

statues, myriads of people filling the galleries and seats around, with the flourish of trumpets as we entered, gave us a sensation which I can never forget and I felt much moved. . . . The sight as we came to the middle where the steps and a chair (which I did *not* sit on) were placed, with the beautiful crystal fountain just in front of it, was magical – so vast, so glorious, so touching. One felt – as so many did whom I have since spoken to – filled with devotion, more so than by any service I have ever heard. The tremendous cheers, the joy expressed in every face, the immensity of the building, the mixture of palms, flowers, trees, statues, fountains, the organ (with 200 instruments and 600 voices, which sounded like nothing), and my beloved husband, the author of this "peace Festival", which united the industry of all nations of the earth – all this was moving indeed, and it was and is a day to live for ever.'

The Times described the proceedings in an almost awe-stricken tone:

'There was yesterday witnessed a sight the like of which has never happened before and which in the nature of things can never be repeated. They who were so fortunate as to see it hardly knew what most to admire, or in what form to clothe the sense of wonder and even of mystery which struggled within them. The edifice,

elow **Views from the gallery on the first**
en day which was for season ticket
lders only.

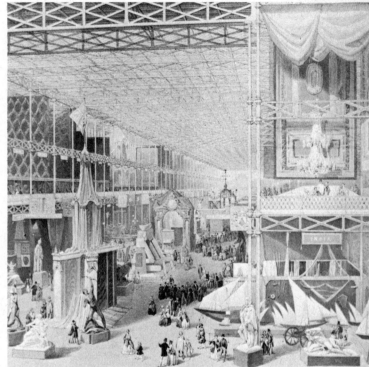

Part of the Machinery Court.

the treasures of art collected therein, the assemblage and the solemnity of the occasion, all conspired to suggest something even more than sense could scan, or imagination attain. There were many there who were familiar with magnificent spectacles . . . but they had not seen anything to compare with this. . . . Around them, amidst them, and over their heads was displayed all that is useful or beautiful in nature or in art. Above them rose a glittering arch far more lofty and spacious than the vaults of even our noblest cathedrals. . . . It was felt to be more than what was seen, or what had been intended. Some saw in it the second and more glorious inauguration of their Sovereign; some a solemn dedication of art and its stores; some were most reminded of that day when all ages and climes shall be gathered round the Throne of their Maker; there was so much that seemed accidental, and yet had a meaning, that no one could be content with simply what he saw.'

One cannot help being struck by the ecclesiastic terminology and religious sentiments that pervade much of the contemporary comment on the Great Exhibition. Queen Victoria was 'filled with devotion' while *The Times* felt a 'sense of mystery' and referred to the Throne of God. The building itself was described in terms of church architecture – the nave, the aisle, and the transept – while the opening ceremony with its organs, choirs, prayers and Hallelujahs resembled a cathedral service. Critics of the Victorians attribute this zealous attitude to a worship of money and materialism. They are wrong. The changes that were wrought through the first half of the nineteenth century were as dramatic and far reaching as those we are experiencing today, but with the difference that while we are jaded to the point of cynicism and boredom, they beheld the manifestations of human intellect with wonder and tried to grasp their true implications. While we posture in front of a sycophantic magic mirror, mouthing meaningless mottoes about man standing

Top Part of the Machinery Court.

Top right The Indian section.

Centre Powers's 'Greek Slave' (see page 57).

Below left Greek and Persian sections.

Below right Egyptian, Turkish and Greek stalls.

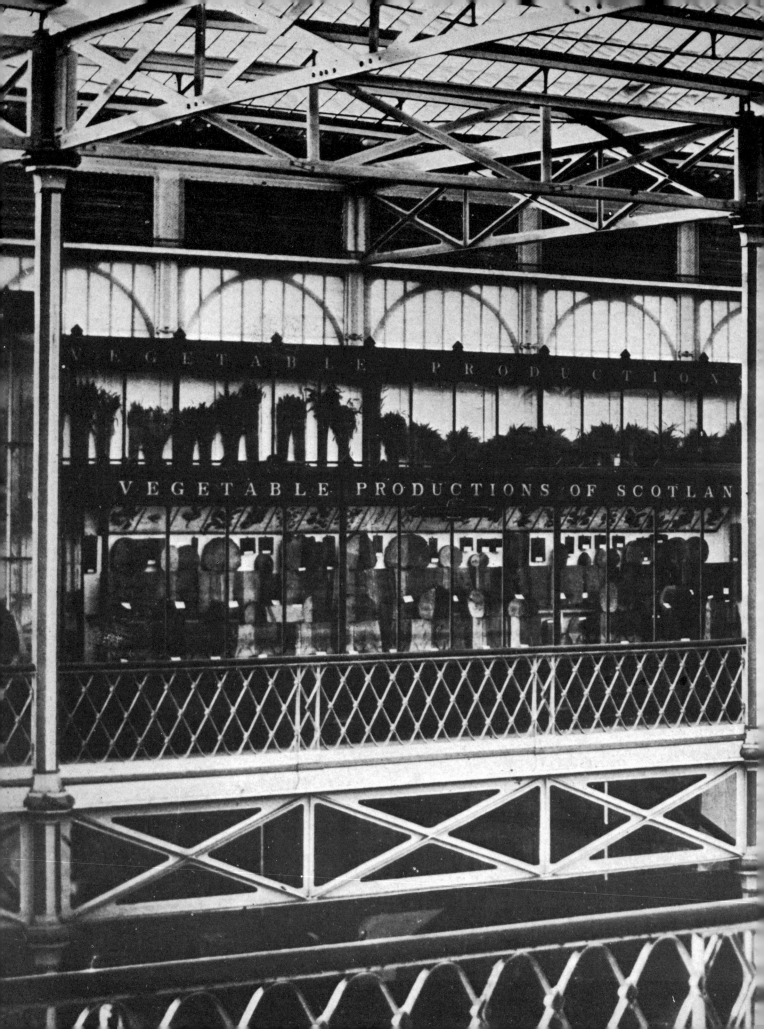

triumphant on the threshold of this age and that age, they remained humble and awestruck. To us their attitude towards scientific and industrial progress seems naïve, but it led to a series of social reforms more drastic and far reaching than any before or since. The movement of reform started by the early Victorians rolled on with gathering momentum for a hundred years with the result that reformers today are left scratching their heads in their search for something to reform. It was not the Crystal Palace and its contents that were reverenced by the people of 1851 but what they stood for. It was described as a 'symbol . . . of mystical significance' and on reflection this description may not be as extravagant as it sounds.

When the opening ceremony was over Alfred Tennyson went home and penned his impressions in verse. In the ecstasy of the moment his Muse forgot that Cole, Paxton or even Prince Albert had ha[?] any hand in the affair for he wrote of th[e] Queen:

'She brought a vast design to pass
When Europe and the scattered ends
Of our fierce world did meet as friend[s]
And brethren in her halls of glass.'

The Queen also felt constrained t[o] commit her emotions to writing tha[t] night. She entered in her diary:

'God bless my dear Albert, God bles[s] my dearest country, which has show[n] itself so noble today. One felt so gratef[ul] to the great God, who seemed to pervad[e] all and to bless all!'
And further on:
'Albert's name is immortalised.'
The Prince was content to record tha[t] the day's events had been 'quite satis[-] factory'. Unfortunately the reflections o[f] Colonel Sibthorpe at this time are no[t] recorded.

Queen Victoria, Prince Albert, the baby prince and the Duke of Wellington at the Great Exhibition.

THE EXHIBITS

'. . . neither crystal nor a palace.
It was a bazaar . . .'

(LEIGH HUNT)

The complete catalogue of the 100,000 objects which formed the Great Exhibition of the Works and Industry of all Nations fills three massive volumes of 500 pages each. The most popular and probably the most beautiful object in the collection was Follett Osler's Crystal Fountain which was made especially for the Exhibition. Occupying the place of honour, where the transept intersected the nave, it was 27 feet high and consisted of 4 tons of pure crystal glass. It became a meeting-place for families and friends visiting the Exhibition and remained so for eighty-five years before it perished with the Palace in the great fire.

In the early days of photography when only the rich could afford to travel, the novelty of other parts and climes could only be experienced by most people through the medium of the magic lantern and the monochromatic illustrated papers. But here it seemed as though in an immense Aladdin's cavern the whole world had contracted into a glorious riot of spectacle and colour. There were silks and satins, furs and feathers, jewelled weapons and saddles, gold and silver ornaments of every kind, clocks, cabinets, couches and chairs, thrones in ivory and zebra wood, adornments in jet, jasper and jade, tapestry, embroidery, lace and brocade, fine linens, leatherwork, gold and silver filigree, perfumes, tobaccos, exotic foods and drinks, pottery, majolica and terracotta, porcelain from Wedgwood, Worcester, Derby, Sèvres, Delft and Dresden, marble and metal statuary, furniture in onyx and carvings in a hundred different woods. These, and tens of thousands of other articles, were scattered in extravagant profusion as if they had been spouted from Osler's magic fountain.

Within a few feet of each other were displayed the exotic offerings of the East and the mechanical and scientific triumphs of the West. The machinery section, or for that matter the entire Exhibition, was dominated by the 'Great Hydraulic Press' which dwarfed even Nasmyth's famous steam-hammer which stood near by. The companies of James Watt and Maudsley showed marine engines; Merryweather his fire-engines and Bessemer his centrifugal pumps. Next to a 31-ton broad-gauge locomotive by Brunel was another powered by four horses treading an endless belt that drove the engine through a series of gears; it was claimed that it had reached 60 mph at its trials. There was a complete coal-pit head fitted with a new device which, if the rope broke, 'prevented the destruction of property'. (Life and limb were not mentioned.) Some machines were ornamented with Gothic tracery and others supported on Doric columns while

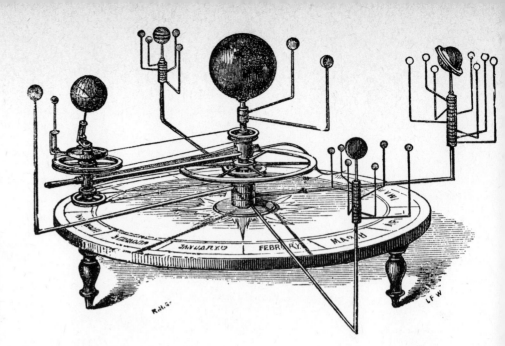

one engine at least was decorated in the architectural style of ancient Egypt. Much of the machinery was kept in motion by belt drives worked by a large mill engine whose boilers were housed in another glass and iron building in the Palace grounds. Outside also were the more ponderous examples of man's work and industry – obelisks, anchors, blocks of marble and granite and a lump of coal weighing 24 tons.

On an empty piece of ground near Knightsbridge Barracks the 'Model Dwelling House' was on view. This was designed under the supervision of Prince Albert himself. It consisted of four self-contained flats, two on each floor, and the building was so designed that it could be multiplied horizontally or vertically to form what we would now call a block of flats. Each unit cost £120 and it was proposed to let them for four shillings a week. Thus, it was argued, capitalism would perform a much-needed social service while securing a return of about 7 per cent. Albert's Model Dwelling House was later moved to Kennington Park where it can be seen today. It is a charming little building and compares very well with many of today's 'accommodation units'.

In the raw materials section were piles of minerals, ores and timber; tusks of ivory, oil-yielding palms and some samples of Welsh gold.

The section devoted to Civil Engineering contained a model of Liverpool Docks, complete with 1600 fully rigged ships; models of bridges, railway layouts, lighthouses and canals, as well as various building contrivances which included a device for carrying smoke from chimney-pots directly into the sewers.

Although the primary purpose of the Exhibition was to promote peace and goodwill between nations, there was a fine selection of aggressive weapons which included naval and military guns, models of warships and a submarine. Also in this section was 'a twelve-shilling rifle specially designed for the purpose of barter with the African native, side by

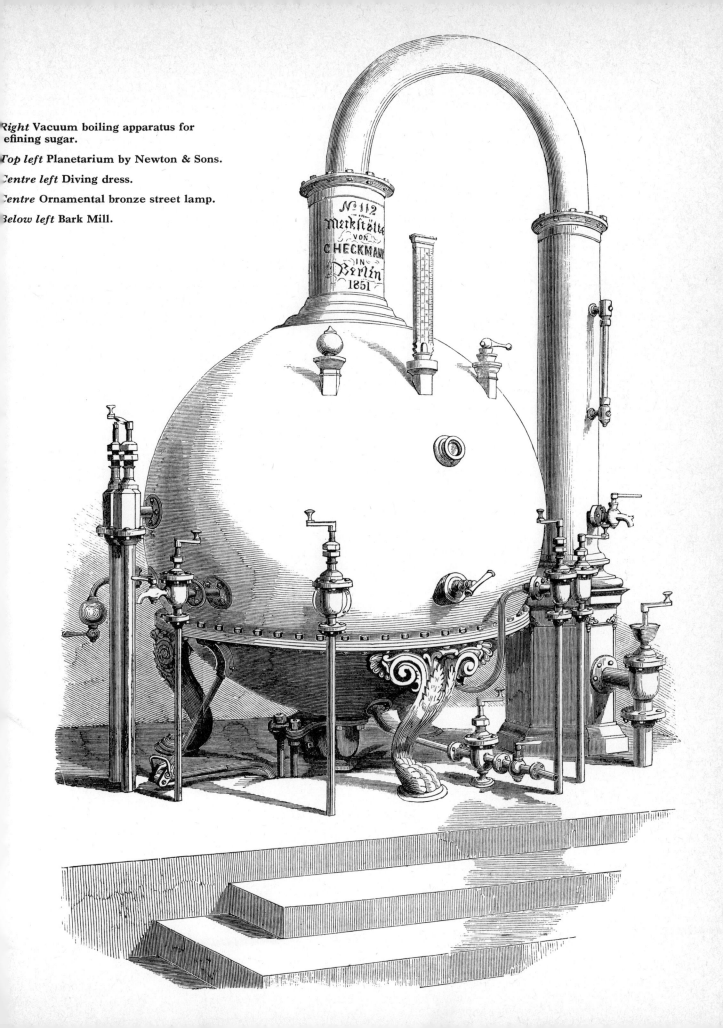

Right Vacuum boiling apparatus for refining sugar.

Top left Planetarium by Newton & Sons.

Centre left Diving dress.

Centre Ornamental bronze street lamp.

Below left Bark Mill.

Above Agricultural implements.

Left The less pilferable goods were kept outside.

Right Column of Cornish granite.

Top right **Agricultural implements.**

Centre **Wood-lagged portable engine and agricultural implements.**

Below **Blocks of Welsh coal.**

side with a totally different model for the purpose of shooting him down'.* Birmingham contributed a splendid array of shackles, chains, manacles, pinions, handcuffs and fetters for export to America's slave States.

In the transport section the horse-drawn vehicle was overwhelmingly predominant. The thousands of years of its development had produced a bewildering variety of types; broughams, basternas, barouches, buggies, britzkas, berlins, curricles, cabriolets, chariots, clarences, chaises, gigs, governess-carts, jaunting-cars, landaus, pony-carts, phaetons, state coaches, traps and unicorns. Near by there was a lifeboat with an ornate figure-head in which could be boiled eight quarts of coffee.

The textile section was so extensive that it was divided into fourteen sub-sections, which in turn were split into sub-subsections. The principal divisions were cotton; woollen and worsted; silk and velvet; flax and hemp; mixed fabrics, including shawls; leather, including harness and saddlery; skins; furs; feathers and hair; paper, including printing and bookbinding; woven, spun, felted and laid fabrics; tapestry, including carpets; lace and embroidery and, finally, articles of clothing. This last subsection included every conceivable article of apparel from cotton aprons and loincloths to ermine

robes and quilted armour. It also contained some that were almost inconceivable such as a safety hat for use in railway travel, 'mathematical' underclothing and corsets that 'opened instantaneously in case of emergency'. A Dumfries hatter offered 'Parisian hats for gentlemen' and another piece of headgear was labelled the 'Patent Ventilating Hat', 'the principle of ventilating being to admit air through a series of channels cut in thin cork, which is fastened to the leather lining, and a valve fixed to the top of the crown, which may be opened and shut at pleasure to allow perspiration to escape.'*

In the section called, rather ominously, 'substances used for food' could be found honey, dates and tamarinds from Egypt; spices, wines and delights from Turkey; oil and macaroni from Tuscany; almonds, olives and figs from Spain and catawoba wine from America. Other wines included Madeira made from malt, sparkling hock from raisins and rhubarb champagne.

The medical section contained bleeding-instruments described as 'substitutes for leeches', artificial legs, arms and teeth, one set of which was fitted with 'a compensating swivel which allows the wearer to yawn without displacing both upper and lower sets'. A 'medical walking-stick' containing medicines, surgical instruments and an enema was

* Hobhouse, op. cit., p. 80.

* Official catalogue.

**Prince Albert's 'Model Dwelling House' –
this building was moved to Kennington
Park where it can be seen today.**

Below Philosophical instruments.

displayed next to a false nose made in silver.
These two marvels of medical science
were too much for one commentator who
wrote of them: 'Would not a small tin
case have answered the same purpose [as
the walking-stick] and far more con-
veniently as it might be put into the
pocket. . . . We will not pronounce rashly
on [the artificial nose] but it strikes us,
that all artificial noses, both in shape, size
and the amount of nose required, will
depend upon the amount wanting by an
individual, and the size and shape, in fact
suited to his particular case; the material
also of which the nose is manufactured
would very often have to be regulated by
the special circumstances.'*

Another medical sample was a pulpit
which could be connected to the pews with
gutta-percha pipes for the use of the deaf,
and Shillibeer, the fashionable Victorian
undertaker, showed his 'expanding
hearse'. There was also an 'expanding
figure of a man', composed of 7000 working parts. This was in the philosophical
instrument section and it won a prize, the
only imaginable reason being that it was
so utterly useless. Also classed as 'philosophical' was a 'charvolant', or carriage
drawn by kites; and a selection of
cameras, barometers and navigable balloons. Other 'philosophical' exhibits included electric clocks, electro-plating
devices and electric telegraphs, in spite
of Brunel's intimation that he wished to
see 'electric machines' excluded from the
Exhibition as he considered them to be
mere toys. (These were strange words
from the man who had pioneered the
adoption of the electric telegraph.) Ross's
great telescope was on show together
with a variety of navigational and astro-
nomical instruments. There was a pair of
'portable steel spectacles' and Russia
sent a quantity of what is mysteriously
described as 'portable soup'. Then there
was the Anhydrohepseterion, a device
which enabled a potato to be stewed in
its own juice; a stiletto, or 'defensive
umbrella'; a knife with 1851 blades; a
galvanized walking-stick which gave a

* *Tallis's History of the Crystal Palace*,
London Printing and Publishing Company,
1855, vol. 1, p. 117.

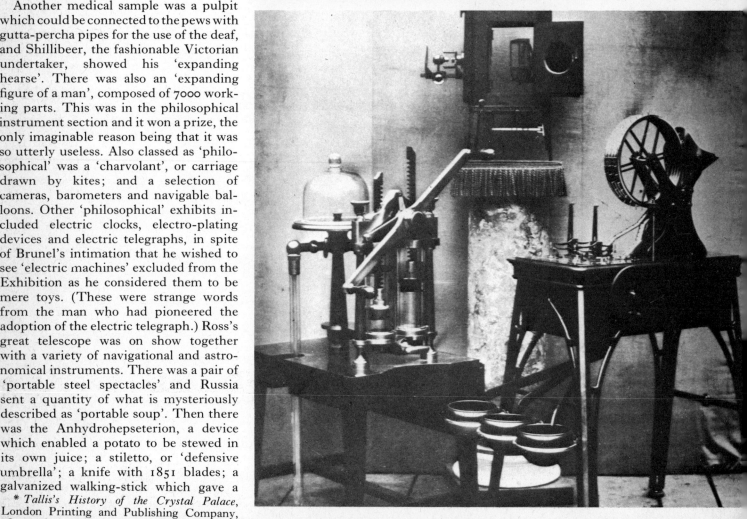

Below left Part of the Indian section.

Centre Steam turbine.

Right Nasmyth's steam-hammer, invented ('after a few minutes' thought', he said) to forge the proposed paddle shafts for the *Great Britain*.

Below Crampton Locomotive.

A penknife with 1851 blades made especially for the Great Exhibition. An example of superb craftsmanship wasted on an article that is neither useful nor ornamental.

slight electric shock if held in one hand and a violent one if held in both; the 'Silent Alarum Bed' which tipped the sleeper on to the floor at a predetermined time; the 'euxesis for shaving without soap or water'; a bird-cage made from 2522 pieces of wood, and a large vase made from mutton-fat. On investigation I find that the mutton-fat was not the jade of that description but was in fact what it claimed to be. There was a very silly collection of 1500 stuffed animals arranged as 'comical, humorous and interesting scenes in animal life'. They included a group of stuffed frogs, one of whom was holding an umbrella, and another called *Schoolmaster Severity* in which a baby rabbit was being bastinadoed by a marten. These tableaux were prepared by a M. Plouquet who apparently had wasted twenty years of his life on the task.

The American contribution was large – too large in fact, for, with their national trait of enthusiasm, the Americans had booked far more space than they could comfortably fill. As a consequence quantity usurped quality and the extra space was filled with stacks of milk-churns, piles of biscuits and mounds of soap. They offered a vacuum coffin guaranteed to prevent decay; a machine for turning over the pages of music; a model of a floating church; a gigantic piano designed to be played by four performers at once and a composite piano and violin which could be played by one. They also sent 6000 fossils, a number of lethal weapons and a stuffed squirrel.

China booked some space but sent nothing. As a result, shops and warehouses all over Britain were combed for examples of Chinese produce. The result was a collection of antiques and junk.

Russia sent a great quantity of stone furniture and a pair of doors in malachite, 14 feet high and price-listed at £6000. Included in Jersey's offering was a paper model of Queen Victoria.

The foregoing is but a brief description of an amplitudinous display exemplifying an age which was riding quite breathlessly on the crest of the wave produced by the impact of the Industrial Revolution. One of the specific aims of the Great Exhibition was 'to improve the application of art and design to industry' – a proposal which had been seen by Colonel Sibthorpe as an invitation to flood the British market with trumpery and trash. To some extent the Colonel was proved right. Trumpery and trash there was in abundance, as we shall now see, but Britain was responsible for at least half of it.

above The 'talking telegraph'. Code symbols, corresponding to those on the keys, appeared on flags from the top of the head whilst the mouth moved meaninglessly. A stupidly useless toy. The batteries are, of course, modern.

right Cast-iron fireplaces.

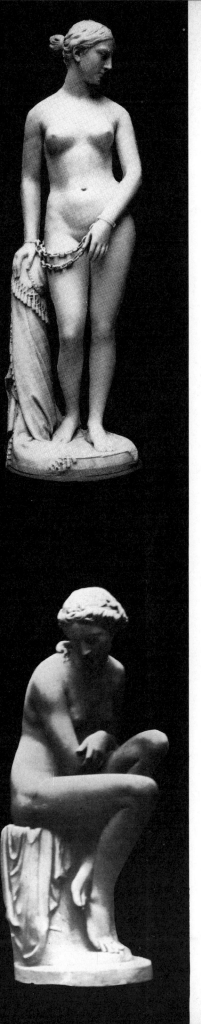

A lot of the statuary was deliberately titillating. 'Andromeda Exposed to a Sea Monster' and the 'Greek Slave' (top row, third and fourth from the left), excruciating in their effrontery, were always the centres of admiring crowds.

7

THE ART

'A man must go out of his way to
make anything really bad'
(AUGUSTUS WELBY PUGIN)

If the Great Exhibition did anything to improve the application of art to industry, which is doubtful, it did so by demonstrating the appalling result of the split that had occurred between art and manufacture and of the greedy attempt to substitute the machine for the craftsman. In addition, the Victorian conviction that their tastes, their habits, their way of life – in fact their whole age had come to stay, constrained them to make everything to last for ever. The harnessing of steam-power and its application to manufacture had aroused in nineteenth-century Europe a striving for more and more mechanical control of the environment and, as a result, every new process was seized and pressed into the service of the factory and applied to the product without regard to aesthetic quality and with a total lack of artistic discipline. This trend had, by the middle of the century, become a rout which destroyed the feeling for Classical form that had lasted for over a hundred years. '. . . the fine arts of 1851, examples of the bastardisation of taste without parallel in the whole recorded history of aesthetics, have come off badly. . . . And if any lesson is to be drawn from the Great Exhibition solely with reference to taste it must be that design in the hands of a machine-minded, money-seeking generation tends to take a downward curve.'*

* Yvonne ffrench, *The Great Exhibition, 1851*, Harvill Press, 1951, p. 230.

One of the visitors to the Exhibition was William Morris, then a youth of seventeen. What he saw appalled him – the lack of respect and sympathy for the materials used, the reckless romanticism and above all the banality of the whole display.

Nowhere was this more apparent than in the furniture section. It seemed as if anything made of wood was passed and repassed through carving machines until not the smallest area of its surface remained flat. The delicately carved leaves of the Regency had proliferated into clumsy clumps of wooden foliage, hideous to behold, and Chippendale's claw and ball feet of ancient Oriental use were replaced by recumbent dogs, eagles' claws and the paws of wild animals. From Ireland came a chair emblazoned with heraldry; it had arms in the form of two wolves, one bearing the legend, 'Gentle when stroked', the other, 'Fierce when provoked'. Towering above the rest of the furniture was a four-poster bed of immense dimensions, so ornate that it even turned the stomach of a hardened contemporary commentator: 'It is more fitted for a corpse to lie in state on, than for a place of repose . . . the footboard is so high and solid that it shuts in the sleeper as in a prison, and completely impedes the free circulation of air.' A commode, made from a number of

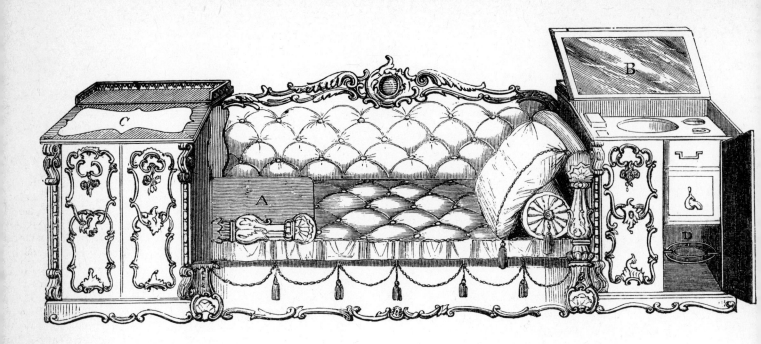

'... in the year 1851, when all that glittering roof was built, in order to exhibit the petty arts of our fashionable luxury – carved bedsteads of Vienna, glued toys of Switzerland and gay jewellery from France – in that very year, I say, the greatest pictures of Venetian masters were rotting at Venice in the rain, for want of a roof to cover them, with holes made by Cannon-shot through their canvass.'*

John Ruskin, *The Opening of the Crystal Palace considered in some of its Relations to the Prospects of Art*, 1854.

different woods, had 'panels ornamented with marqueterie and carvings and painted china in the centre; the whole finished with rich gilt mouldings'.

A peculiarly repulsive chair made from papiermâché and described as 'The Day Dreamer' was 'decorated at the top with two winged thoughts – the one with bird-like pinions and crowned with roses representing happy and joyous dreams, the other with leathern bat-like wings, unpleasant and troublesome ones. Behind displayed Hope under the figure of the rising sun.' Very highly rated was the Kenilworth Buffet' – an enormous piece that had been hewn out of a huge oak at Kenilworth Castle. Said the *Art Journal*, 'any attempt to describe this elaborately carved piece of workmanship, would, in our limited space, be out of the question' – an observation with which we may sympathize.

Next to the furniture section was the 'Mediaeval Court', designed by Augustus Pugin, a Catholic convert and champion of the Catholic revival in England. Through the medium of the medieval formalism that he loved, Pugin designed the Court as a propaganda booth for Catholicism and many complaints were made against it. Even before the Exhibition opened, the Prime Minister had written to Prince Albert on the subject and the Prince replied that he had already prevented the Belgians from exhibiting waxworks representing the Pope and twelve of his Cardinals as a setting for a display of Brussels lace. 'But', he went on, 'I cannot prevent crucifixes, rosiers, altar plate, etc. etc. . . . those who object to their idolatrous character must be relieved to find Indian Pagodas and Chinese Idols in other parts of the Exhibition.'

Scattered profusely throughout the building were sculptures and statuary contributed by distinguished artists from all over the world. Subjugating the rest through sheer power and massiveness was *The Amazon*, a spectacular group cast in zinc and bronze by the Prussian sculptor, A. Kiss. In its way it was a magnificent piece but it gave a taste of what was to come, for most of the sculpture was in the worst form of narrative art. A great deal of it was frankly carnal, if not deliberately titillating, being representations of desirable young females ripe for ravishment. Most of them lacked clothes but all lacked artistic integrity. *The Veiled Vestal*, *The Circassian Slave Exposed in the Market* and *Andromeda Exposed to a Sea Monster* were among the most brazen of the stone hussies who coyly seduced the imaginations of the maturer visitors and it is to be hoped that there were not too many gentlemen visitors wearing the Patent Ventilating Hat, otherwise the assembly would have resembled a rally of steam-engines with open blower-valves. The libidinous appeal of *The Veiled Slave* was admitted by one observer: 'We confess ourselves no advocate for that style of art', he leered, 'which avails itself of the beauty of the female form for the purpose of exhibiting

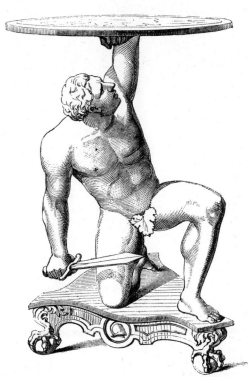

Mrs Partington's Teaparty

PLOUQUET - Stuttgart

Schoolmaster Severity

High Victorian Art.

Left Dog protecting child.

Right Child caressing his Defender.

Centre left 'The Amazon.'

Below left 'The Lion in Love.' 'Love love when you hold us we may well say goodbye to prudence.'

Below right 'Greek Hunter.'

Left Two examples of Plouquet's 1500 stuffed animals arranged as 'comical, humorous and interesting scenes in animal life'. They travelled to Sydenham with the Palace and, mercifully, perished in the fire.

the debased consequences of the misplaced power of her natural protector.'

Andromeda Exposed to a Sea Monster is excruciating in its effrontery. As a piece of vulgar eroticism it compares well with the photographs of female flesh exhibited outside today's disreputable cinemas and it had the added advantage of being three-dimensional.

Hiram Powers's *Greek Slave* made a great impression and was the constant centre of a crowd of admirers. It stood under a red velvet canopy in the middle of the American section. The catalogue said: 'The artist has delineated a young girl, deprived of her clothing, standing before the licentious gaze of a wealthy Eastern barbarian. Her face expresses shame and disgust at her ignominious position, while about her lips hovers that contemptuous scorn which a woman can so well show for her manly oppressor.'

The poet Samuel Warren was overcome with emotion when he beheld the *Greek Slave*. Scalding tears must have fallen on to the paper when he wrote:

'Look ye yourselves upon her loveliness!
Ponder her thrilling tale of grief! –
She is not mute, O marble eloquent!
She pleads! She pleads!'

Other popular trollops looking no better than they ought to be were *The Startled Nymph*, *Titania*, *Psyche* and *Eve with the Serpent*.

The rest of the sculpture was mawkishly sentimental, including such items as *The Unhappy Child*, *Boy Attacked by Serpents*, *The First Step* and *The Mourners*. As the best example of sheer debauched taste, *The Lion in Love* won, paws down.

For ballast the sculpture collection contained a 21-foot-high statue of Queen Victoria in bronze, another of her mounted on a charger, the Prince of Wales as a shepherd and a marble carving of a group of billiard players.

Mr Goggleye a Country Gent.n reads all about the "Great Exhibition of 1851!

Mr Goggleye arrives in London on the 1st of April to visit the Exhibition! and is very much perplexed, to find in which of the above localities, it is held.

He finally discovers it in Hyde Park, which very much surprises him, for he thought. The TIMES! and Lord Brougham, had, come to the determination, of not permitting it!.

He pays his Shilling. & purchases

A CATALOGUE! of the Exhibition.
The following works, are those, noted, and marked as the most remarkable, by Mr Goggleye. Viz

No 100
French Works.

No 81
A New Stove, and OLD FUEL, for Heating! the Houses of Parliament.

No 150
A Screw.
That was made to last about three years; but it is now supposed, will never wear out.

N 1100
IRISH INDUSTRY!
Specimen of Irish Manufactured Wearing apparel.

No 2000
Glasses, for enabling every body to take the same view of everything, so that there never will be no disagreement on nothing!!

No 21040
A design for an Equestrian Statue of the Duke! by Master Tommy H'ORSESA

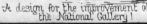

No 10000
A Working Model of a Press. Suitable to the pressure of the times.

No 32050
A design for the improvement of the National Gallery!

No 90723
A project for building Castles in the Air!

No 20318732.
Plan of a proposed line, through the Earth to the Antipodes, with Telegraph communication to all the planets, by professor Airey.

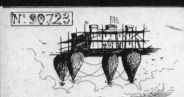

No 27080717
A Machine for extracting SUNBEAMS from CU—cumbers.

No 9007327172
Piece of Tough YARN! Spun by a Sailor.

No 7202022
Plan for removing the Statue, from Hyde Park Corner.

No 200700000
CALIFORNIAN GOLD
IMPLEMENTS, for 'raising the wind'.

No 9723 0172
London Fashions.
Chapeau de Printemps
Ladies Corset & dress Expander.

No 3784000
British Industry!
Silk, drawn & spun by hand.

No 37601901
THAMES Fever FILTH CHOLERA DEATH
A plan showing that the present system is the best for Draining London! — of its population!

No 81700235
Designs for Art Manufactures.

No 50730020
Weights & Measures

Chimney Ornaments.

No 9178203100
COMMON SENSE
A nut shell, in which is contained an infallible specific for the cure of Cant, and Humbug.

No 90000000000, and last.
A New Work! invented and designed for the Exhibition of 1851 by Timy Takemin

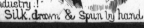

'Mr Goggleye's Visit to the Exhibition' –
a satirical booklet published in 1851. The
world's problems have changed little since
Mr Goggleye's day.

THE VISITORS

'A lady in Bloomer attire made her
appearance . . . and the new cos-
tume, and the fair wearer of it, as
may be imagined attracted no small
share of attention'

(*The Times*)

The Great Exhibition was open to the
public from 1st May to 11th October and
during that period it received over
6,000,000 visitors – an average daily
attendance of 42,831. On one day there
were over 93,000 people in the building
at the same time. To avoid crushing, the
official guide requested visitors, 'in going
through the building, to follow as much
as possible the course of the sun'.

On the shilling days the humble people
flocked to London from the provinces by
special excursion trains, carts and carriages or on foot. Rustics who had never
before travelled beyond the vicinity of
their villages scraped together a few
shillings and 'did' the Exhibition. They
wandered through the aisles and galleries
in gazing wonderment at objects of whose
very existence they had never dreamed.
They must have looked with awe at the
mighty moving machines and probably
with envy on the rugs, the china, the
stuffed birds and wax fruit and flowers.
They were interested in the textiles, fas-
cinated by the agricultural machines but
baffled by the philosophical instruments.
Mingling with the country people were
the cloth-capped artisans who, perhaps,
showed more interest in machine tools,
looms and building contrivances. But one
and all spent some time gaping at the
fabulous Koh-i-noor diamond which was
displayed in the centre of the jewellery
section.

On these shilling days the atmosphere
in the Palace was a festive one, of best
clothes, delighted children and bags of
sandwiches. Messrs Schweppes had paid
£5500 for the privilege of running the
four large refreshment-rooms and during
the run of the Exhibition they sold
1,092,337 bottles of mineral water as well
as oceans of tea and coffee.

Of the shilling day visitors Thackeray
wrote, unkindly and not very cleverly:

'Amazed I pass
From glass to glass
Deloighted I survey 'em;
Fresh Wondthers grows,
Before me nose,
In this sublime Musayum.'

The Admiralty granted six days' paid
leave to its workers in Portsmouth Dock-
yard to give them an opportunity of seeing the Exhibition and several business
houses gave their clerks four days' leave
together with a few pounds spending
money.

On Saturdays, which were five-shilling
days, the building was crowded with
middle-class families. Almost as acquisi-
tive as their modern counterparts, they
lingered over the furniture and domestic
appliances, estimating the costs (no prices
were displayed) of chairs and tables,
candelabra, chandeliers, 'appliances for
cooking by gas', bathtubs and those new-
fangled contrivances, water-closets. So

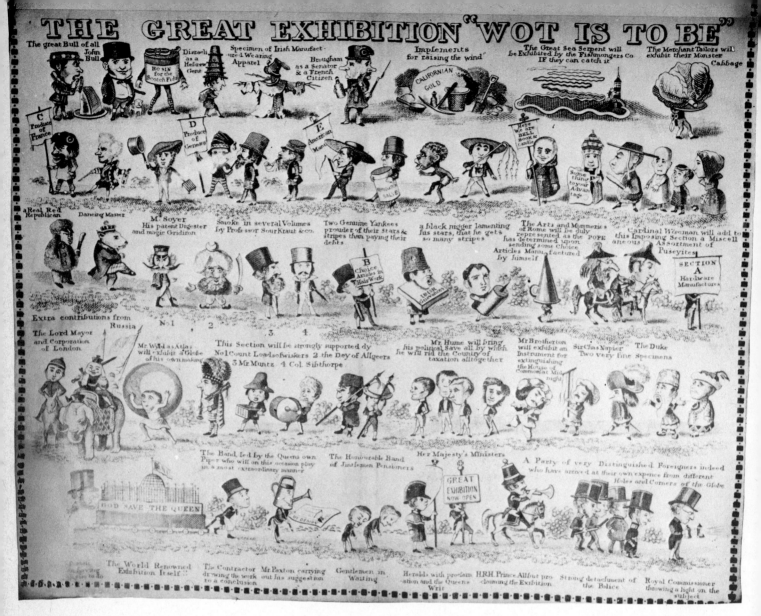

Satirical cartoon printed on silk for the opening of the Great Exhibition.

crowded did the building become on Saturdays that it was proposed to allow Sunday opening. The reaction against this was immediate and was, of course, spear-headed by the Member for Lincoln. 'Is it true', he roared in the House of Commons, 'that a work of art has been seriously damaged from being photographed on a Sunday?' The scheme was abandoned.

Charles Dickens made several visits but he found it too overwhelming, complaining that he was not sure that he had seen anything but the Crystal Fountain and *The Amazon*. When the future King Edward VII was taken he was so delighted with some wax effigies of the murderous Thugees of India engaged in their art that he wrote glowingly of them in his diary. The entry was read by his father, Prince Albert, and the poor boy was severely reprimanded and told that he was 'born in a Christian and enlightened age in which such atrocious acts were not even dreamt of'.

The Queen never tired of the show. She made twelve visits in the month of May alone. On one occasion she admired a glass vase engraved with allegorical figures and asked the Exhibitor the meaning of one scene which depicted a huge eye peeping from the sky at a boy who was jumping from a boat to the land. 'The Boy, Madam,' explained the proud stallholder, 'is the Prince of Wales; the Eye is the Eye of God looking out with pleasure for the moment when His Royal Highness will land on his kingdom and become the reigning Sovereign.'* Another regular was the Duke of Wellington who liked walking among the stalls by himself. On 7th October, when there was a record attendance of 110,000, he was recognized by a huge concourse of admirers who advanced along the nave towards him. For a while the Iron Duke stood resolute, facing the oncoming horde, and then, for the first time in his long, ferocious life, he turned his back and ran.

* Wemyss Reid, *Memoirs and Correspondence of Lyon Playfair*, Cassell, 1905, p. 121.

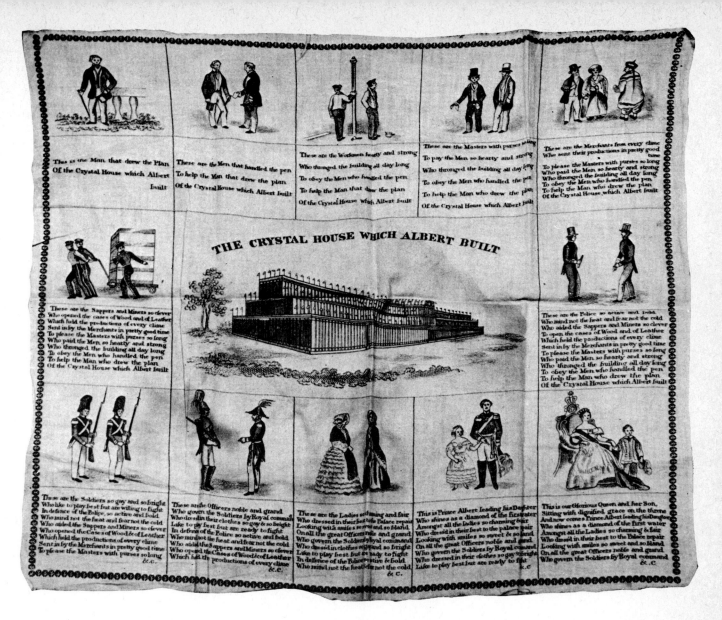

Crystal Palace poem printed on silk.

After the 6,039,195th visitor had passed through the turnstiles, the Exhibition was closed to the public on the evening of 11th October. On the 13th and 14th it was open to the Exhibitors and their friends and on the following day there was a simple closing ceremony which included a short speech by Prince Albert and a rendering of the 'Hallelujah Chorus'. The Great Exhibition was at an end.

As a show it had been a huge success but in its aims it was a complete failure. It did not improve trade to any marked degree, neither did it improve international relations or further the cause of peace. It certainly did nothing to improve taste in industry, but it *did* make a profit. After awarding Paxton £5000 and settling all outstanding accounts, the Commissioners were left with £180,000. In addition, nearly £100,000 worth of the exhibits were presented to them. It was decided to purchase Gore House and 22 acres of land near the Brompton Road and to erect there a permanent exhibition building to house the gifts, together with other objects which, in the opinion of the Commissioners, exemplified good taste and design. This was the beginning of the centre of art and learning that still flourishes in South Kensington. It now includes the Victoria and Albert Museum, the Science Museum and Library, the Natural History Museum, the Geological Museum, the Imperial Institute, the Royal College of Science, the Royal School of Mines, the City and Guilds College, the Royal College of Art, the Royal College of Music, the Royal College of Organists and the College of Needlework. The list can be continued. This, then, is England's legacy from the Great Exhibition.

The Press wrote its obituary with near-reverence and the following paean is typical: 'The tale of Hyde Park in 1851 will fall on the page of history. Fallen thrones will lie around it: here the Saturnalia of power – there the wild excess of popular freedom . . . everywhere

Left Scene – Exhibition Refreshment Room
Visitor. 'Pint o' Beer, Miss, please.'
Miss. 'Don't keep it. You can have a
Strawberry Ice and a Wafer!'

Right A Hint to the Commissioners.
'Mon Dieu, Alphonse! Regardez-donc.
Comment appelle-t-on cette Machine-là?'
'Tiens, c'est drôle – mais je ne sais pas.'

Below Country visitors to the Exhibition.

Below A shilling day.

Bottom Her Majesty as she appeared on 1st May, 'surrounded by horrible conspirators and assassins' ('Punch').

anarchy, repression, conspiracy, darkness, dismay, and death. In the midst of all these struggling spirits rises up the great figure of the Crystal Palace, to redeem the age.' The official report of the Commissioners was concerned with more prosaic matters and amongst a bewildering array of statistics it solemnly recorded that during the run of the Exhibition 827,820 persons paid for the use of the 'waiting-rooms' and 'in addition a larger proportion of gentlemen used the urinals, of which no account was kept. No apology is needed for publishing these facts which [demonstrate the] sufferings which must be endured by all, but more especially by the females on account of the want of them.'

Referring to Powers's *Greek Slave*, the late Christopher Hobhouse wrote:

'[In] the work of an American sculptor in Rome, imitative in design, meretricious in execution, and deliberately tittivating [*sic*] in its sentiment, is represented and embodied the two supreme shortcomings of the period – its vulgarity and its eclecticism. The possibility of the appreciation of the fine arts had spread downwards to the middle-classes; and the middle-classes had gone bald-headed for all the artistic fallacies – nature, pathos and moral purpose. But we need not for all that despise the early Victorians. Where they suffered from a surfeit of ill-digested knowledge and ill-controlled idealism, the present day shrinks in diffident self-consciousness from any form of allusiveness or didacticism. Where they were adventurous, we are cynical; where they were dogmatic and hearty, we are merely empty and apologetic. The meanness and timidity of modern design, the cult of the second-rate, attained their climacteric, let us hope, in the reign of Edward the Eighth, and found their most characteristic expression in the postage stamp of that monarch. The reaction is due to come.'*

Hobhouse wrote these words in 1937 – a time which, in some respects, can now be called 'the good old days'. The reaction is still overdue.

* Hobhouse, op. cit., p. 137.

A 'Punch' impression of public reaction to
the news that the Palace was to be removed
from Hyde Park. The benign-looking
gentleman portrayed in the lower line,
second from the left, is, of course, Colonel
Sibthorpe.

HEADS OF THE PEOPLE ON THE REMOVAL OF THE CRYST

"WELL, I DON'T SEE ANY EARTHLY USE IN
IT REMAINING. WHY, THERE'S THAT BACK
ROOM I HAVE NEVER LET SINCE IT HAS BEEN
OPEN!"

"IT'S VERY INSTRUCTIVE, I CON-
FESS; BUT IT LOWERS THE NEIGH-
BOURHOOD DEUCEDLY: IT HAD BETTER
COME DOWN!"

"LOR!—EX'BITION CLOSED; AND I
WITHIN THREE-HALFPENCE OF THE
SHILLING!—BLOW IT!"

"LOR!—I WONDER WHERE THEY'LL
PUT THE HUGE LOOKING GLASS?"

"THE CRYSTAL PALACE COMING DOWN!—
LOR BLESS ME!—WHAT A PITY!—GREAT
SHAME!"—&c., &c.

"COME DOWN?—TO BE SURE, MY BOY;
WITHOUT, INDEED, THEY TURN IT INTO A
CASINO. THEN!—AH, THEN!"—&c., &c.

ALACE.

"Lor, John, what a Pity!"
"My Dear Girl, the Annoyance is really dreadful!"

"Come Down?—Of Course!—Should never have been Raised!—Ruination to Business!" &c., &c.

⑨
THE TRANSFORMATION

'A cucumber frame between two chimneys'

(JOHN RUSKIN)

When the doors of the Great Exhibition finally closed there remained only the clearing up. This included the awarding of medals to the prizewinners and knighthoods to Fox, Cubitt and Paxton. Cole was made a Companion of the Order of the Bath. The Hyde Park site had to be restored to its original state and from this the controversial question arose, 'What is to become of the Crystal Palace?' This had become a problem when the beauty and popularity of the building was apparent, and now that the Exhibition was over it had become urgent. One wit suggested that 'it should be kept under glass'. Paxton, naturally enough, was loath to see the end of his masterpiece and during the summer of 1851, with the Exhibition in full swing, he was at the head of a movement to leave the Palace in Hyde Park and turn it into a 'Winter Park and Garden under Glass'. In a pamphlet on the subject he wrote:

'In this Winter Park and Garden the trees and plants might be so arranged as to give great diversity of views and picturesque effect. Spaces might be set apart for equestrian exercise, and for carriage drives; but the main body of the building should be arranged with a view of giving great extent and variety for those who promenade on foot. Fountains, statuary, and every description of park and garden ornament, would greatly heighten the effect and beauty of the scene. . . . Beautiful creeping plants might be planted against the columns, and trailed along the girders, so as to give shade in the summer, while the effect they would produce by festooning in every diversity of form over the Building, would give the whole a most enchanting and gorgeous finish.

'Besides these may be introduced a collection of living birds from all temperate climates, and the science of Geology, so closely connected with the study of plants might be illustrated on a large and natural scale, thus making practical Botany, Ornithology, and Geology familiar to every visitor.'

In July 1851 Paxton put the scheme before Parliament in the form of a petition and secured a reprieve for the building until May 1852 by which time, he was told, a decision would be made.

When Colonel Sibthorpe learned that it was proposed to leave the Crystal Palace where it stood he could hardly believe the evidence of his own senses. This is clear from the inspired heights of eloquence to which he rose in opposing the Motion on 29th April 1852. Beginning quietly with a masterpiece of understatement he rose to a perfectly balanced climax which flowed to a dignified finish.

'I have', he began, 'on several occasions expressed my opinion upon this so-called

**Plan of the Winter Park and Garden
under glass as it was when
it was first opened.**

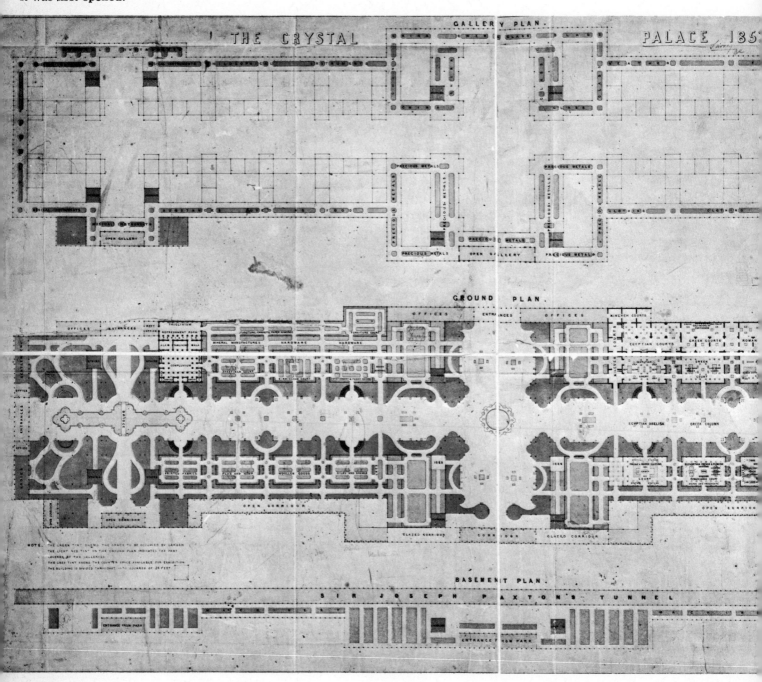

The Park and its contents in 1864.

Crystal Palace, and I believe my conduct has been in strict conformity with those declarations. I have never entered it. If anybody offered me a thousand guineas . . . I would not enter the place. No! upon principle, I would not, I *dare* not enter it. The very sight of it almost sickens me. I have not desired to see any act of violence resorted to, or the law transgressed, in order to demolish it, but I own that nothing would have given me greater pleasure than if, by some superior power to that of man, it was annihilated at one fell swoop, and no trace left of the gross delusion. . . . Who benefited from it? Not one. . . . Foreigners and contractors were the gainers. The poor people are drawn from their distant homes, and from their honest occupations, to see this big bauble. They are trapanned, seduced, ensnared and humbugged out of their hard earnings. . . . By their fraudulent insinuations and promises, they have wrung the shillings out of the hands of the poor and sent them back to their families penniless. They [the Government] have had their Exhibition, I believe – for of course *I* never saw it – stuffed with foreign fancy rubbish. Show and tinsel are nowadays preferred – cheap and nasty – whilst our solid durable English manufacture is neglected. The Crystal Palace is a transparent humbug . . . the sooner the thing is swept away the better; and as for the public, I believe . . . [that they] regard it in the same light as I do – as a common nuisance. I am in favour of affording recreation to my fellow creatures of all classes, but I will never subscribe to perpetuate such an unmitigated humbug as this . . . I prefer the interests of my fellow countrymen to that of foreigners. I will give my decided opposition to the Motion.'

As Colonel Sibthorpe enjoyed considerable support on this matter the Motion was defeated. Fox and Henderson on being served with notice to remove the building, which was now their property, began to look about them for a market for the iron and glass.

Paxton was saddened by the decision

 CONTINUED ON PAGE 79

Breakfast-time at the Crystal Palace,
Sydenham.

Dinner-time at the Crystal Palace.

Building the south water tower.

Below left The south wing seen from the roof of the main building.

Bottom left The building from the terrace.

Right The south wing.

Bottom right The north end from the reservoir.

The Transformation

Extreme left **First ribs of the nave.**

Left **The terrace and south tower.**

Following pages: top left **Building the Great Transept.**

Bottom left **End of the terrace and north tower.**

Top right **The south end.**

Bottom right **Brick piers for the columns.**

but not dismayed. Foreseeing the probable outcome of his Hyde Park scheme he had been busy with an alternative and he had already raised £500,000 to form a company to buy the building together with a new site on which to erect it. The place chosen was an area of 200 acres of wooded parkland on the summit of Sydenham Hill – then a quiet country spot – commanding one of the finest views near London. The Palace was purchased from Fox and Henderson for £70,000 and on 5th August 1852 rebuilding began.

The Sydenham Crystal Palace was, to say the least, larger than the Hyde Park structure. The latter had been built for little more than £150,000 and now Paxton had half a million pounds to spend – although, after the purchase of the site, the balance had to go a long way. Apart from the cost of the original structure it had to be transported to Sydenham, rebuilt and furnished as a Winter Park and Garden. Digby Wyatt and Owen Jones were sent abroad to ransack the world's great art collections and make plaster casts of the choicest of the statuary to furnish the series of courts they had designed to demonstrate the art and architecture of all the great civilizations. Trees, plants and flowers, some of them very rare, were bought by Paxton for the 200 acres of park, and for the inside of the Winter Palace he purchased, at great cost, a famous collection of palms and other plants that had taken Messrs Loddiges of Hackney over one hundred years to assemble. The grounds were to be transformed into one enormous garden, the slopes, hollows and swelling mounds to become lakes, fountain basins, reservoirs, sweeping avenues and stately terraces. There were to be flower temples, pleasure walks and shrubberies and both Park and Palace were to be amply decorated with the statues, busts, urns and vases that were already arriving from Wyatt and Jones on the Continent.

Paxton envisaged a system of fountains that would rival Versailles and this involved the building of two tall towers

The south transept from the second terrace.

to supply the necessary head of water. As to the Palace itself, Paxton, free for the first time in his life from the considerations of surrounding architecture, confinements of space and the restraint of patrons, designed a building that made the original seem modest in comparison.

The new site sloped down steeply to the east, leaving Paxton no alternative but to add a basement storey. Then, on Barry's suggestion the flat roof was vaulted from end to end and, so that this arch did not detract from the prominence of the transept, the latter was greatly enlarged and doubled in width. This involved the adding of two more storeys which, in their turn, entailed a considerable increase in the width of the nave. The transept was now so large that Paxton decided that two end transepts were necessary to balance it and these required the addition of two wings. In this way the simple three-storeyed building grew into a complex five-storeyed one with a total floor area (including galleries) of 843,656 square feet and a capacity of nearly 44,500,000 cubic feet – nearly half as much again as the original. The result of this was an area of glass amounting to some 1,650,000 square feet. It was no wonder, then, that before the building was half completed the £500,000 capital was exhausted. The Crystal Palace Company issue, however, had been well oversubscribed and there was no difficulty in raising more money. The final cost of the whole undertaking was £1,300,000, which included the following: The building had cost £235,240; the water towers, wings and heating equipment £123,532; the hydraulic works £80,085; while the Park and outside works cost £340,231. The remainder went on the land, the interior decorations and arrangements and on the exhibitions of sculpture and fine arts.

Osler's Crystal Fountain was there, still in the place of honour under the now swollen central transept and from there, running down the north nave, was the series of Fine Art Courts, each one illustrating a particular period in the

history of art. There being nowhere else to put it, Pugin's Mediaeval Court had been brought to Sydenham along with the Palace and it was now joined by the Grecian, Roman, Byzantine, Romanesque, Pompeian, Chinese, Alhambra, Renaissance and Egyptian Courts. Viewed together, these Courts constituted a unique illustration of the development of architecture, sculpture and mural decoration from the earliest times to the sixteenth century, so that the visitor '. . . might gain, in practical fashion, an idea of the successive stages of civilisation which have from time to time arisen in the world, have changed or sunk into decadence, have been violently overthrown, or have passed away, by the aggressions of barbarians, or the no less degrading agency of sensual and enervating luxury'.

In the Egyptian Court, Sphinxes, obelisks and a collection of artificial mummies were brooded over by full-sized reproductions of two colossal statues.

The Grecian Court was built in the style of a Temple of Jupiter containing examples of Greco-Roman and Classical sculpture while the Assyrian Court overwhelmed the visitor with colossal bulls and columns. In the tropical department Paxton put pomegranates, oranges, lemons, palms and exotic flowers. Round the ornamental fountains he planted his favourite lily and to add to the luxuriance he arranged vines to climb and spread across the ferro-vitreous roof. There was an aquarium, a gallery of paintings, a library and reading-room, a Court of the Kings and Queens of England, a Hall of Fame and a theatre in which was played everything from Greek Drama to Variety and Pantomime. There was also a Concert-room with 4000 seats and under the central transept was the Grand Orchestra which could accommodate 4000 musicians and which was built round a Great Organ with over 4500 pipes.

In the Natural History collection were models and tableaux of the various races

The south transept from the second terrace

Right **The gardens and the south transept.**

CONTINUED ON PAGE 92

Left The open colonnade.

Below The central transept from the garden.

Following pages Inside the nave, south end.
The nave looking north.

ft The nave from the north end.

low The fall of the scaffolding for the first
ir of the Great Transept ribs. Twelve
en died in the accident.

low right The upper gallery with the
ill's eye' girders.

ttom left Steam-power in the Great
ansept.

ttom right Casting a Sphinx on the
race of the south transept. The
hinxes can still be seen.

Erecting the Grand Orchestra in preparation for the opening ceremony.

and ages of man together with hundreds of stuffed birds, beasts and fishes.

The Palace was flanked to north and south by the two water towers that supplied the fountains. Built by Brunel, they were 284 feet high* and each held aloft a tank, 47 feet in diameter and 38 feet high, holding 300,000 gallons of water. Through the centre of each tower ran flues which carried the smoke and fumes from the furnaces, boilers and steam-engines which raised the water to the tanks. The foundations of the towers needed the greatest care in their construction as the towers with their load each weighed 3000 tons and they were built on the sloping side of a clay hill. In the event of the bursting of a pipe a large quantity of water might have been discharged to cause a slip in the surrounding ground, so Brunel carried his foundations down to a considerable depth where he laid a large base of Portland cement; on this he built a cone of brickwork rising to ground-level. The towers were twelve-sided with two hollow cast-iron columns at each angle. They had ten storeys and on each floor was a strong wrought-iron diaphragm, 5 feet wide. Brunel did not consider it prudent to use any of the columns as water-pipes lest the expansion resulting from the temperature should cause unequal support to be given to the tanks. The system of fountains extended across the terraces and throughout the grounds and consisted of ten basins, the largest of which threw its jets to a height of 150 feet. There were also a number of water temples and waterfalls and when the whole system was in operation nearly 12,000 jets played using over 7,000,000 gallons of water an hour. The gardens were laid out with lakes and islands, a maze, a grotto, a rosary, groves, temples and lawns, and at the Cascade Temple visitors could contemplate a symbol of Abundance gushing from the feet of Fortune. In the lower part of the ground there were, and still are, 'a series of those

* A firm of toilet-roll manufacturers demonstrated the length of their product through an advertisement that pictured a customer on top of one of the towers. He held one end of an unrolled tissue. The other end touched the ground.

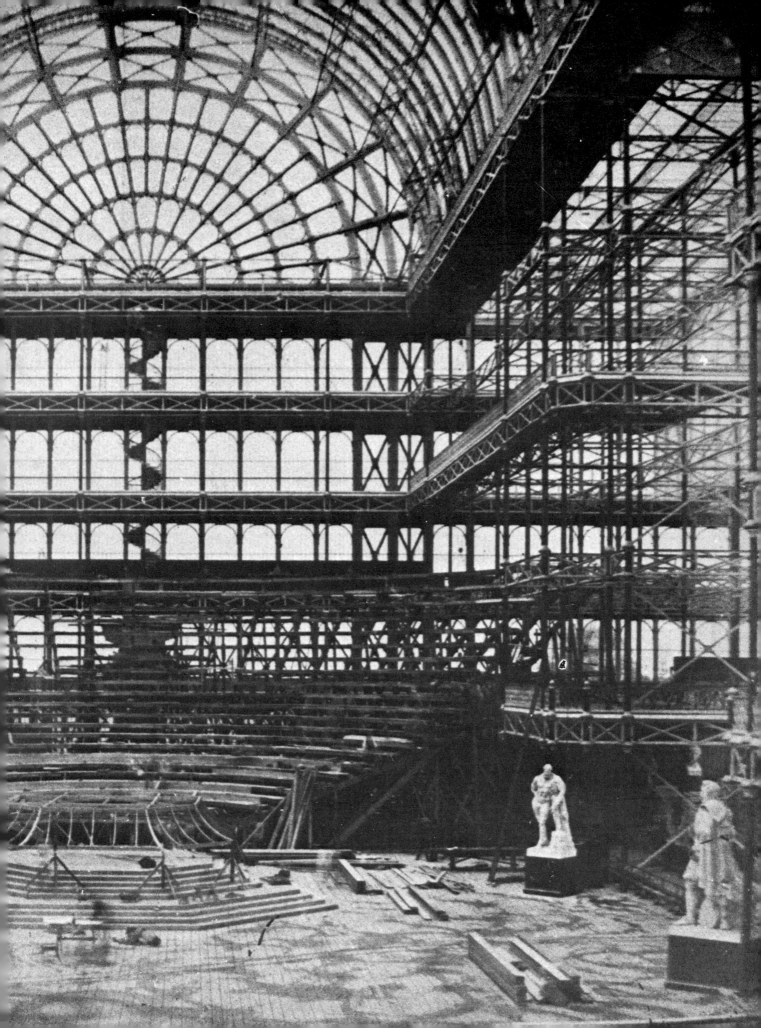

Below left Workshop of the Egyptian Court

Below left **Workshop of the Egyptian Court**

Below right **Erecting casts in Pugin's Mediaeval Court.**

Right **Building a marine tank.**

Bottom right **Finishing the Egyptian tomb.**

vast and unpleasant animals that existed on our planet fortunately before man made his appearance'.* They included the iguanodon, the plesiosaurus and the pterodactyl, and their creator, Professor Owen, was entertained to dinner by the Palace Directors in the belly of the iguanodon, after which he delivered an address from that monster's skull.

The Sydenham Crystal Palace was due to be opened in June 1854, but in the early part of that year the Directors were disconcerted by the arrival of a letter signed by '13 eminent persons'. There can be little doubt that some of these gentlemen, having visited the Great Exhibition and admired the pornolithic creations of contemporary artists, obtained less pleasure from the innocent naturalism of Classical sculpture. The letter read:

'We the undersigned, desire the directors to accept our assurance that we address them in no unfriendly spirit regarding the present condition of the

nude male statues of the human form prepared for exhibition in the palace.

'We are persuaded that the exhibition to promiscuous crowds of men and women of nude statues of men in the state there represented must, if generally submitted to, prove very destructive to that natural modesty which is one of the outworks of virtue, and which a great French writer has called "one of the barriers which Nature herself has placed in the way of crime . . ."

'We, the undersigned, have grounds for declaring that a strong feeling is rising upon the subject, and that, unless this slight concession is made, the matter will be so resolutely brought before the public in London and in other parts of the kingdom that everyone will be driven to form a decided judgement on the point; and it is our fixed expectation that such an agitation will prove very damaging to the Company. . . .

'We, the undersigned, only add that we should deeply regret to see the fire of

* V. R. Markham, *Paxton and the Bachelor Duke*, Hodder and Stoughton, 1935, p. 242.

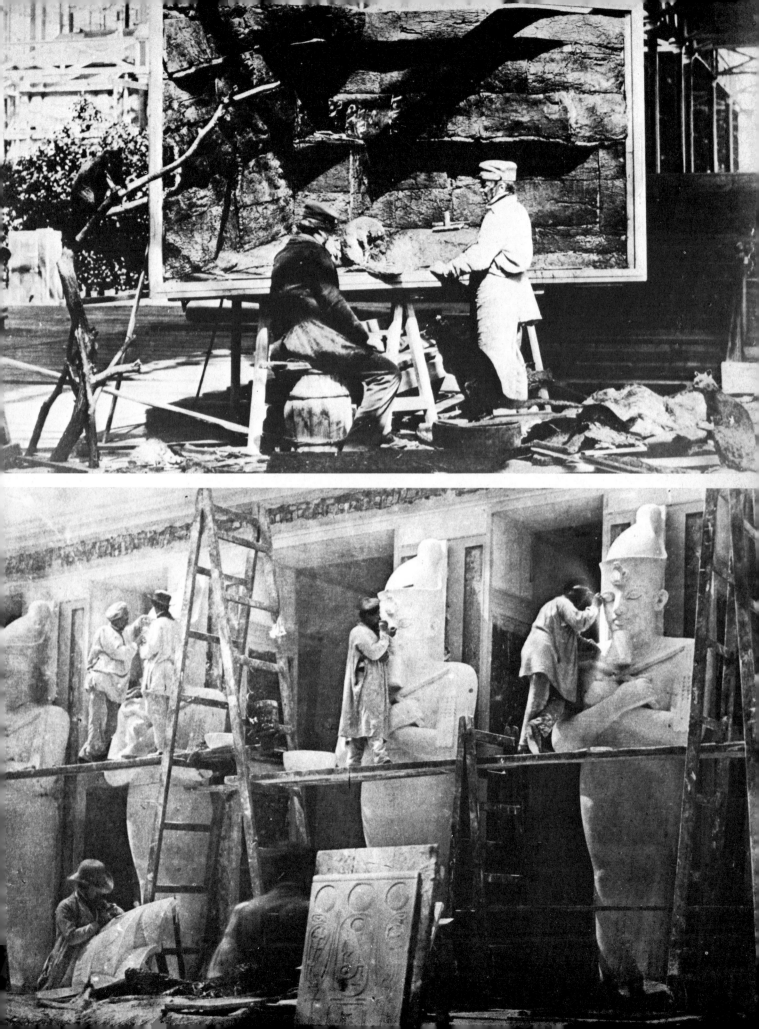

Left **Interior of Alhambra – Court of the Lions.**

Right **Exterior of the Assyrian Court.**

Bottom left **Exterior of the Alhambra Court.**

Bottom right **Exterior of Nineveh Court.**

public remonstrance opened in full force against the magnificent undertaking . . . [which we] regard as a national glory.

'We demand but a small thing . . . the removal of the parts which "in life" ought to be concealed, although we are also desirous that the usual leaf be adopted.'

The threat was unmistakable and the thirteen persons making it must have been powerful as well as eminent for the Directors panicked and capitulated – much to the fury of Owen Jones and Digby Wyatt. The operation of removing the virility of the offending Deities was simple enough and was performed by the deft but indelicate application of hammer and chisel. The covering of the resultant wound, however, presented problems, for on 8th May with only a month to go before opening, *The Times* reported that the Directors were having difficulties in finding 'a supply of fig leaves for the nude statues'. The plaster foliage was eventually found or manufactured and riveted on to the emasculated loins of the heroes of old but even this did not assuage the outraged susceptibilities of a group of hostile clergymen. The battle continued past the opening date and well into the year, but by 15th December the Directors had had enough. In a letter to the Rev.

...ntrance to the tomb of Beni Hassan.

Right Building the Greek Court.

Extreme left **Colossal head of Bavaria.**

Left **Plinth for the Colossi of Abu Simbel.**

Centre **Building up the Colossi of Abu Simbel.**

Right **Painting the Colossi of Abu Simbel.**

Following pages **The Crystal Palace in its halcyon days. 'A Winter Park and Garden under Glass.'**

The Grand Avenue, terraces and gardens.

C. Herbert of Burslem they wrote that a Committee had been formed to 'examine the works of art throughout the palace, with a view to the draping of all statues which could be justly considered offensive to delicacy', and that this having been done they 'beg to inform you that it is not their intention to do any more than they have already done in this matter'.

The Palace and its grounds took nearly two years to complete and, as can be seen from the picture on page 107 which gives an impression of its enormous size, this was a considerable achievement. A serious mishap occurred in August 1853 when the scaffolding for the Great Transept collapsed causing the deaths of twelve workmen. But in spite of this, the building was opened on time by the Queen on 10th June 1854 in the presence of 40,000 people and became an immediate popular success.

If the Great Exhibition was a microcosm of Victorian industry then the Sydenham Crystal Palace was one of Victorian leisure. At a time when museums, galleries and parks were few it offered Londoners the opportunity to expand their knowledge of the world while relaxing in lovely surroundings. They could contemplate the splendid rural view of Kent and Surrey, ponder on the monsters that towered amongst the trees, picnic in the woods or on the lawns – and all within a few minutes' journey from the centre of the city. For the children there was the Great Maze, the Underground Grotto, the playgrounds and the boating-lake and, when it rained, there was the Palace itself – too vast to become crowded and yet almost overflowing with a bewildering variety of things to see, all calculated to delight, instruct, astonish and amuse. It is easy for us to smile when we consider the attraction that this farrago of eclectic bric-à-brac held for the Victorian masses, but a hundred years ago the Crystal Palace was unique in that it offered, for a few pence, a whole day's entertainment of a kind which hitherto had only been within reach of the well-off.

The Crystal Palace

The Grand Avenue, terraces and fountains.

10

THE WINTER PALACE

EMMA (*entertainingly*). That's the
Crystal Palace.
THOMAS. Is it?
HARLEY GRANVILLE-BARKER, *The
Madras House*, Act 1)

The Sydenham Crystal Palace was a great popular success although due to Paxton's prodigality and the resultant high cost of upkeep it was never a profitable enterprise. During the first thirty years an average of 2,000,000 people a year made their way to the top of Sydenham Hill and, to cope with this traffic, two new railway lines were built. The Brighton Company united its lines from London Bridge, Victoria and Kensington at the low-level station which was connected to the Palace by a 720-foot-long glass-covered colonnade, the walls covered by creeping plants and lined with the now ubiquitous plaster statuary. The London, Chatham and Dover Railway delivered its passengers at the high-level station which was connected directly to the Palace grounds by a charming brick-vaulted tunnel running underneath the building. The tunnel can be seen today. Later a pneumatic railway was built in the grounds to connect the Sydenham and Penge entrances – a distance of about 600 yards.

The Palace's popularity continued until the end of the century when, sadly, it began to wane as habits changed and other amenities became available. But during the second half of the 1800s it drew more and more visitors as it added more and more to its various attractions. A Great Marine Aquarium, over 400 feet long, was built there in 1872. Then there were Schools of Art, Science, Literature, Music and Engineering. It was at the Crystal Palace that, for the first time ever, a large audience watched moving pictures, for in 1868 a huge Zoetrope, turned by a gas engine, was installed which showed a programme that included *The Conjurer, The Acrobat, The Umbrella Man* and *Jim Crow*. Then there was a parrot house, an aviary, a monkey house, a club, an orangery and a Victoria Cross Gallery. Balloon ascents were a regular and favourite attraction and, of course, M. Blondin made a visit and cooked an omelette on a high wire. It was the ideal place for shows and exhibitions and they followed each other with ever-increasing frequency – rose shows, pigeon and poultry shows, goat shows, rabbit shows, cat and dog shows, trade fairs, electrical exhibitions, art exhibitions, aeronautical, mining and photographic exhibitions and in 1896 an exhibition of horse and horseless carriages. The permanent courts, exhibitions and attractions were situated along the sides of the building and in wings. The special exhibitions were held in the main body of the building, in the galleries and in the grounds. It became the place for massed meetings of societies of every shade and description: the National Temperance League, Scottish Athletes, German Gymnasts,

CONTINUED ON PAGE 110

eft Queen Victoria (centre) opening the
*y*denham Crystal Palace.

ight The Palace and gardens from the air.
*t*he north transept and wing were destroyed
*b*y fire in 1866 and were never rebuilt. This
*p*hotograph was taken by a balloonist.

Left The south tower from Westow Hill, Upper Norwood, in the 1890s.

Bottom left The nave and transept looking south showing the 'ridge and furrow' construction of the roof.

Right Crystal Palace Parade and the high-level railway line which brought visitors from all parts of London.

Left The water temple.

Centre The fountains.

Right The main entrance illuminated with flares.

Bottom right The Palace in the 1930s.

Salvation Army, Police, Firemen, Oddfellows, Foresters and a thousand others. Then there were concerts, music festivals, massed bands, circuses and pantomimes. Particularly popular were the pantomimes of John M. East who also produced spectacular shows in the Palace grounds. The most famous of these was *Invasion* and every performance drew at least 25,000 spectators. It was carefully timed to begin just before dusk fell. On the open space in front of the terraces a full-size village was built complete with shops, church and school. When the show started the village became alive with people going about their business, some in carriages or on horseback, while the children danced round a Maypole in the school playground. Then a regiment of soldiers (in reality they were local Territorials) marched through the street drawing guns. As dusk fell a spy was detected by the police and locked up – then, as it became really dark, the drama began. The spy escaped and made signals to the sky. Then a Zeppelin appeared over the village and dropped bombs on the school and the church. From the ruins came the screams of trapped and dying children. An invading army dropped *by parachute* from the Zeppelin and a full-scale battle was fought over the ruins of the village between the invaders and the home army. The Zep-

pelin flew away, the enemy was surrounded and captured and the victorious British troops marched off the field to the music of a full brass band. To put on *Invasion* meant that the whole village had to be reconstructed for every performance.

The price of admission, usually one shilling, varied on these special days – on one day 30,000 paid a guinea each to attend a flower show. On these occasions it appears that the railways, with their customary lack of foresight, never provided enough first-class accommodation for the middle-class and upper-class passengers who attended these functions. Sir William Hardman wrote in his diary in 1862:

'Yesterday we went, according to annual custom, to the Dramatic Fete at the Crystal Palace. I had four ladies to take charge of, and managed the difficult operation satisfactorily . . . I am no judge of numbers but I have estimated the visitors at about 25,000. The Railway Company were much to blame for the utterly insufficient supply of first-class carriages. The admission at the Palace being 2/6, of course very few if any of the passengers took second-class tickets and none *third-class*: yet did the second and third-class carriages exceed the first in number, and we, having taken first-class returns, went to the Palace in a third-

class open at the sides (sheep truck is more appropriate name for it) and returned in a third-class carriage.'*

CONTINUED ON PAGE 125

* S. M. Ellis (ed.), *A Mid-Victorian Pepy* Cecil Palmer, 1923, p. 151.

Left Half a guinea would buy a lady the freedom of the Palace for eight months.

Right The south wing and tower.

Bottom The main entrance in 1935 – the year of King George V's Silver Jubilee.

Below One of the fountain basins in the
1930s. The fountains no longer worked and
many of the basins were dried up.

Centre The lower terrace.

Bottom Part of the gardens.

Below The boating-lake.

Bottom left Song cover, 1864.

Bottom centre For decades every Thursday night was firework night.

Bottom right Contrary to legend, Blondin did *not* perform on a wire stretched between the two towers.

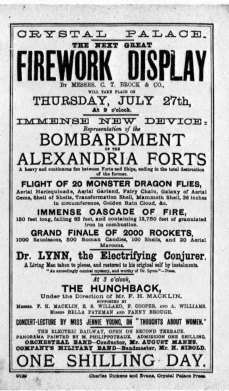

Left Osler's Crystal Fountain moved to Sydenham with the Palace.

Below Song cover in honour of Garibaldi's visit to the Palace in 1864.

Right Kaiser Wilhelm II reviewing the fire brigade in the Palace grounds.

Bottom left The visit of the Shah of Persia.

Bottom right Visit of the Emperor of Russia.

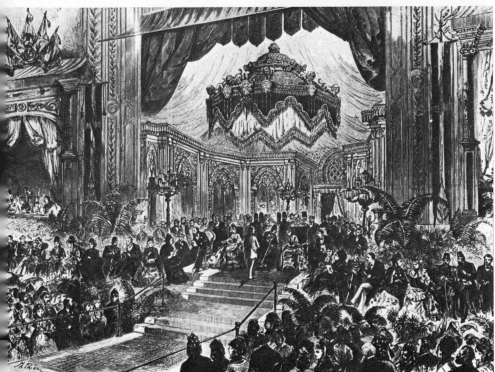

Below Generations of Victorian balloonists ascended from the Palace.

Right Leona Dare was a renowned aerial acrobat. She 'created a profound sensation' all over the world.

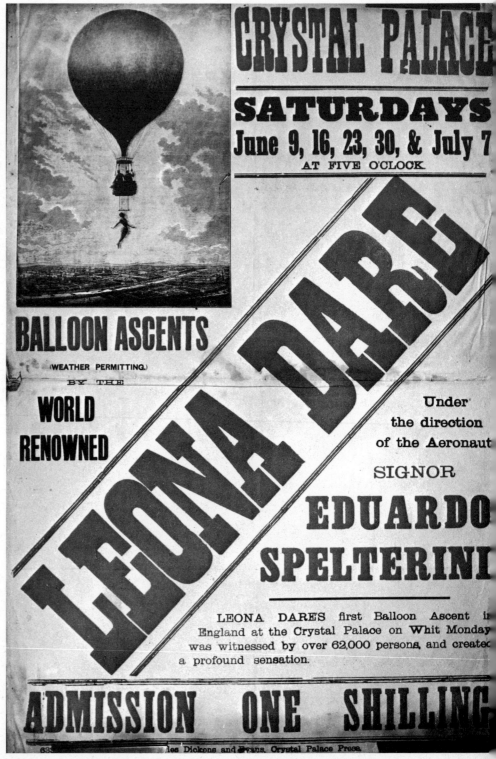

Top left A trial of fire engines in the Palace grounds.

Bottom left The basket of Nadar's balloon, 'Giant', on exhibition in the Palace in 1863. The basket contained a saloon, captain's cabin, photographic dark-room, lavatory and, for a reason unexplained, a printing-press. There was a sun deck above the basket.

Below right Bill for a typical day's entertainment at the Crystal Palace.

CRYSTAL PALACE.

SATURDAY, 25th, and MONDAY, 27th JULY, 1863.

ROYAL DRAMATIC COLLEGE.

A GRAND FÊTE AND FANCY FAIR.

The Council have the honour to announce that they have made arrangements with the Directors of the Crystal Palace for the Annual FÊTE and FANCY FAIR in aid of the funds of the Dramatic College, for the above dates.

THE FANCY FAIR, FAIRY POST OFFICE, WHEELS OF FORTUNE, AUNT SALLY'S,

&c., &c.,

Will be presided over by the following Ladies and Gentlemen, who have kindly tendered their services:—

Mrs. STIRLING.	Miss CARRA NELSON.	Mr. LEWIS BALL.
Mrs. HENRY RUDDELL.	Miss SARA NELSON.	Mr. W. WORBOYS.
Miss KATE CARSON.	Miss AGNES BURDETT.	Mr. J. B. JOHNSTONE.
Mrs. ALFRED MELLON	Miss MARIA SIMPSON.	Mr. DALTON.
(Late Miss Woolgar.)	Miss ESTHER JACOBS.	Mr. JOSEPH ROBINS.
Miss FANNY JOSEPHS.	Miss MITCHELL.	Mr. HOWARD PAUL.
Mrs. BILLINGTON.	Miss KATE RIVERS.	Mr. W. H. EBURNE.
Miss H. SIMMS.	Miss MORELLI.	Mr. W. SHIRLEY.
Miss KATE KELLY.	Miss LAVINE.	Mr. C. BILLINGTON.
Miss E. JOHNSTONE.	Miss PATTI JOSEPHS.	Mr. C. RICE.
Miss AVONIA JONES.	Miss G. TURNER.	Mr. G. HONEY.
Miss L. MURRAY.	Mr. J. B. BUCKSTONE.	Mr. R. JOHNSON.
Miss AYLMER.	Mr. H. COMPTON.	Mr. G. FREE.
Miss E. LIFFDEY.	Mr. FRANK MATTHEWS.	Mr. R. GARDEN.
Miss R. BUFTON.	Mr. J. L. TOOLE.	Mr. J. JOHNSTONE, jun.
Miss TAYLOR.	Mr. PAUL BEDFORD.	Mr. CONWAY.
Miss MINNIE DAVIS.	Mr. E. PHILLIPS.	Mr. CONWAY, jun.
Miss FANNY HUNT.	Mr. JOHN NEVILLE.	Mr. PAUL HERRING.
Miss KATHERINE HICKSON.	Mr. J. G. SHORE.	Mr. TOM MATTHEWS.
Miss LATIMER.	Mr. F. CHARLES.	Mr. MORELLI.
Miss KEGWORTHY.	Mr. ALFRED WALLACE.	Mr. DYAS.
Mrs. HOWARD PAUL.	Mr. R. THORNE.	Mr. FITZPATRICK.
Mrs. CONQUEST.	Mr. T. THORNE.	Mr. SEFTON PARRY.
Miss CONQUEST.	Mr. J. SEFTON.	Mr. J. KIMBER.
Miss C. SAUNDERS.	Mr. R. ROMER.	Mr. FREDERICK OLIVIER.
Mrs. LYDIA THOMPSON.	Mr. H. WIDDICOMBE.	Mr. R. SOUTAR.
Mrs. Sr. HENRY.	Mr. ADDISON.	Mr. T. W. PAULO.

The opening of the Fair by Proclamation.—The Herald, Mr. R. ROMER.

A Thrilling Melo-Drama of the Good Old Bartlemy Fair Times, By OBUJANO, M.M.C., Author of "The Spanish Girl, or the Spy of Naples," "Alfonso and Claudina the Faithful Spouse, or the Fated Race" &c., illustrated by the Real Players (Metropolitan Members of the Profession), at

RICHARDSON'S THEATRICAL SHOW,

ENTITLED

BARBADAZULO VANAGLOROSO,

THE DEMON OF THE CASTLE HEIGHTS; OR, THE BROTHER'S REVENGE.

WITH DOUBLE CAST.

	1st Cast.	2nd Cast.
Barbadazulo Vanagloroso	Mr. J. L. TOOLE.	Mr. R. THORNE.
Bobo de Nazziniento	Mr. J. G. SHORE.	Mr. SOUTAR.
Segnidoro	Mr. E. DYAS.	Mr. F. CHARLES.
Amoroso	Mr. F. OLIVIER.	
Lagrimoso	Miss PAULINA BEDFORD.	Mr. T. THORNE.

Bartlemy Ghosts.

Difunta Primera	Mr. W. H. EBURNE.	Mr. ALDRIDGE.
Difunta Segunda	Mr. J. SEFTON.	Mr. PAULO.
Difunta Tercera	Mr. BEANCONI.	

Dresses by Mr. S. MAY, of Bow Street; Scenery by Mr. T. THOMPSON; Music by Mr. R. ISAACSON. General Manager—NELSON LEE, Esq. Stage Manager—Mr. R. PHILLIPS (Adelphi Theatre).

PARADE.

Parade Master ... ... Mr. C. H. BROOKES. Clown ... ... Mr. PAUL HERRING.
Combatants ... ... Messrs. R. GARDEN, J. B. JOHNSTONE.
The LECLERCQ FAMILY and the LAURI FAMILY.

WOMBWELL'S MENAGERIE.

Astounding Collection of Trained Performing Wild Animals.

Van Amburgh—Mr. J. ROBINS. Principal Keeper—Mr. ADDISON. Mr. LE BARR. BROTHERS WARNE. The Brothers Tanner's Dogs and Monkeys. Brass Band by ISAACSON. Gorilla—Mr. MARTINI (the Original Man-Monkey).
The Parade will be under the direction of the celebrated Mr. W. H. PAYNE and Family.

TEMPLE OF THE ROAD TO HAPPINESS,

Where Ladies may see their Future Husbands, and Gentlemen their Future Wives, by Conseu German, from Kissengen.

BERRY'S WONDERFUL LIVING CURIOSITY—A TORTOISE-SHELL TOM CAT.

WHITE LILIES OF THE PRAIRIE, with their Celebrated NEGRO ENTERTAINMENT.

THE GIPSY TENT, BY MISS AGNES BURDETT.

JACK AND THE GREEN.

My Lord—Mr. C. J. SMITH. My Lady—Mr. R. ROMER. Clown—Mr. C. H. STEPHENSON.

THE GHOST! THE GHOST! THE GHOST! THE WAXWORK!! THE WAXWORK!!

COMBINATION OF ATTRACTION.

The Paul-y-Toole-y-Technic Institution united with the Original Madame Tis-So's. Proprietors, Messrs. TOOLE & PAUL BEDFORD.

STARTLING ILLUSIONS. MECHANICAL FIGURES LIFE SIZE.

THE DIVING BELLE! DISSOLVING VIEWS!

A LECTURE every quarter of an hour, by Professor TOOLE, written by Messrs. BYRON, E. L. BLANCHARD, W. BROUGH, and HALLIDAY.

Admission to the Entire, ONE SHILLING!

"Men should be what they see'em."—*Shakspeare.*

ZADKIEL'S CRYSTAL BALL—"DANCE OF DEATH" AND LIFE—Superior to the Guards' Ball or the Ball of St. Paul's.

WONDERFUL GENEROSITY—Each party entering this Exhibition will be presented with a Full-size Figure (elegantly costumed) of Mr. J. L. TOOLE, as "Assanta," the Gipsy Queen—worth more than the price of admission.

SIGNOR LOGRENIA'S TROUPE OF PERFORMING BIRDS & MICE.

THE ROYAL PUNCH & JUDY—By Mr. H. RIVERS, of the Olympic Theatre.

THE BAND OF THE CRYSTAL PALACE COMPANY.

For numerous other attractions and arrangements of Programme, see future announcements.

ADMISSION, on SATURDAY 2s. 6d., Children, 1s.; on MONDAY 1s. Change can be had at the Fancy Fair, close to the Stalls.

Tickets of admission to the Palace may be had of Mr. J. W. ANSON, at the Office of the College, No. 20, Tavistock-street, Covent Garden; Mr. SAMS, Royal Library; Mr. St. James's Street; Mr. MITCHELL'S, No. 33, Old Bond Street; Messrs. KEITH, PROWSE, & Co., Cheapside; Book-stalls, Great Western Railway, and all stations on the line; at the Crystal Palace Office, 2, Exeter Hall, Strand, and the usual Agents.

B [1130] C. Printed by R. K. BURT, Holborn Hill, City.

TICKETS TO VIEW CAR

Exterior of Italian Court.

Pugin's English Mediaeval Court.

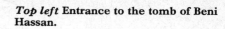

Top left Entrance to the tomb of Beni Hassan.

Bottom left Entrance to Egyptian Court.

Top centre Entrance to Renaissance Court in course of construction.

Centre The Renaissance Court.

Bottom centre The Pompeian Court.

Below The Roman Court.

Bottom right Entrance to the Court of Lions, Alhambra Court.

Extreme left Tropical plants in north wing with entrance to Assyrian Court in the background.

Left 'The First Whisper of Love' by Calder Marshall, RA.

Below Stuffed animals: 'The Bear Hunt'.

Bottom Cleaning the statuary in preparation for the reopening after the First World War.

Left **The Grand Orchestra and the Great Organ.**

Bottom left and right **Championship boxing and wrestling matches were held at the Palace in the 1930s.**

Below **A corner of the organ loft.**

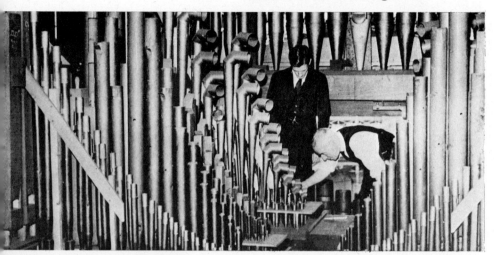

1. Signal Maroon.
2. Special Illumination of the Great Fountain Basin.
3. Rockets . . . emitting Stars of Various Colours.
4. Ascent of two Large Balloons, bearing torches and Aerial Fireworks.
5. Triple Device; Three Fountain Basins, from which spring to a great height Jets of Gold.
6. The Chameleon and Protean Clouds, produced by Twelve Volleys, each of Three Large Shells.
7. Flight of the New 'Royal York' or 'White Horse' rockets.
8. Fire Portrait of Emile Zola with motto 'Welcome'.*
9. Flight of Six Fiery Pigeons from and to their cote.
10. Flight of New Princess May Rockets.
11. Double Device: the Two Great Revolving Suns.
12. Pyrotechnic Water Lilies floating on the surface of the lake.
13. Aquatic Forest of Floating Trees of Fire.
14. Firework Jugglery by Floating Roman Candles.
15. Divers and Skimmers, emitting shrill cries as they dart below, above and on the surface of the water.
16. Device: The Colossal Fountain of Brilliant Silvery Fire.
17. Salvo of Large Shells, 25 inches in diameter.
18. Aerial Festoons of Jewels, released from special Parachute Rockets.
19. The Grove of Jewelled Palms.
20. The Nest of Aquatic Birds.
21. Swarm of Gold and Silver Fireflies.
22. The Pearls of Light, discharged from Batteries of Brock's Special Roman Candles.
23. Signal Maroon.
24. Magical Illumination by Masses of Variously Coloured Fire.
25. Grand Finale Bombardment from opposing shores of the Lake, and Melee by a multitude of Shells, Rockets, Saucissons, Mines, etc. etc.

* Zola was visiting England at the time.

Royalty loved the place. Queen Victoria was a regular visitor and so was Prince Albert until the time of his death. Napoleon III turned up in 1855 ('What a place for a fête', remarked that fun-loving monarch); so did the Sultan of Turkey (1867), the Khedive of Egypt (1869), the Shah of Persia (1873), Tsar Alexander II (1874), the Sultan of Zanzibar (1875), the King and Queen of Greece (1876), and the Kaiser himself (1891).

In 1859 the first of the Handel Festivals was held with a chorus and orchestra of 4000. The famous Crystal Palace firework displays were begun in 1865 and they became a regular summer-night feature which by the end of the century had become world renowned. On the occasions of the Grand Displays some 5 tons of material were consumed and, in a set piece, over 7 miles of quickmatch was used. Small gas balloons were sent up and released magnesium light and fireworks; flights of 5000 or more rockets were set off to discharge plumes of fire and gold and silver stars. The Palace speciality was the famous 'Niagara of Fire', a magnificent fiery cascade which covered an area of 25,000 square feet and burned a ton of iron filings. The programme of fireworks for 23rd September 1893 was a typical one:

CONTINUED ON PAGE 132

Below Programme for Easter Monday 1899. All these events together with the run of the Palace and grounds were offered for one shilling.

Right Firework crowd for a 'Brock's Benefit Night'. The favourite vantage point was the restaurant balcony which can be seen below the transept.

CRYSTAL PALACE
EASTER MONDAY

THE FREE ENTERTAINMENTS are on a scale of magnitude and magnificence unattainable at any other place of Amusement in London!
COME EARLY AND STAY LATE!!
CONSTANT TRAIN SERVICE all day and all the evening.
ONE SHILLING admits to the Palace and to all the Special Shows.
SIXPENCE SAVED by purchasing Railway Ticket including admission.

UNPRECEDENTED ATTRACTIONS.
THE BEST OF EVERYTHING!
Unsurpassable and Unapproachable Programme!!

GREAT
FOOTBALL MATCH
Corinthians *v.* Notts Forest.
(THE FINAL TIE CUP HOLDERS).
Can be witnessed by Tens of Thousands of Visitors without Extra Payment.

Champion Cycle Races
On the Fastest Track in the World.

First Heat **CENTURY CUP RACE**
A. A. CHASE *v.* R. PALMER.
(Under N.C.U. Rules. Permit granted by London Centre).

Re-Appearance of Platt-Betts.
PLATT-BETTS *v.* **5-MILE RECORD**
C. G. WRIDGWAY
versus THE ONE HOUR MOTOR TRICYCLE RECORD.

MOTOR & HUMAN PACING
Tens of Thousands can witness the Races without Extra Payment.

MONSTER
Balloon Ascent
By Mr. SPENCER.
No Extra Charge. Can be witnessed by Tens of Thousands of Visitors.

DANCING All Day
ON THE LAWNS AND DANCING PLATFORM.
SPECIAL BANDS.

MAGNIFICENT DISPLAY OF
FIREWORKS!!
OF UNPRECEDENTED BRILLIANCE
By Messrs. C. T. BROCK & Co.
Can be witnessed by a Hundred Thousand Visitors without Extra Payment.

MUSICAL FIREWORKS! SPORTING FIREWORKS! COMIC FIREWORKS!
LIVING FIREWORKS! FIREWORKS FROM BALLOONS!
SALVOES OF MAMMOTH SHELLS! BATTERIES OF ROMAN CANDLES!
THOUSANDS OF ROCKETS! TONS OF COLOURED FIRE!
P.T.O.

Below The Zeppelin-shaped object cannot be explained – even by Mr Benjamin Brock. Today it would be identified as a flying saucer.

Right A living firework. The overalls were of asbestos.

eft Grand Finale.

entre left Battle of Manila Bay.

ottom left Eighty years a Queen.

Bottom centre Fire picture – Boer War.

Bottom right Fire portrait of Baden-Powell.

The Crystal Palace

Below The tropical department.

Top right Ruins of the tropical department after the north wing burned down in 1866. Neither the wing nor the plants were ever replaced.

Centre right The north transept after the fire.

Bottom left Stuffed animals and ethnographic group.

Below Engine turntable at the high-level
station. Crystal Palace was then the end of
the line.

Bottom Miniature railway, *circa* 1865.

26. The Fairyland Glimpse, by the discharge of Three Magnesium Shells.

Most elaborate and spectacular of all were Brock's famous set pieces. Charles Thomas Brock started them in 1865 as quite small affairs, some 12 feet long, but over the years they were increased in size and complexity and reached a climax with the Battle of Trafalgar which was no less than 820 feet across. Every naval battle of any importance was, at one time or another, reproduced in fire on Sydenham Hill. The last one was the Battle of Jutland which had to be seen to be believed. As huge battleships, outlined in fire, bombarded each other from opposite sides of the lake, the explosions of the shells were reflected in the water as they might have been at sea. Ships blew up and slowly sank and the spectacle ended with the Union Jack, picked out in fire, waving triumphantly over the whole scene. Throughout the seventy years of Brock's Crystal Palace firework displays there was never a serious accident or injury.

An advertisement in 1866 described the Crystal Palace as 'without precedent or parallel, one blaze of decorative art' and another announced that on 1st January 1867 the Rev. H. M. Hart was giving a lecture in the Palace on 'Fire, what causes it, how it is extinguished.' The Rev. Hart never gave his talk for on the night of 30th December the decorative art in the north transept was literally ablaze. The Alhambra, Assyrian and Byzantine Courts, the Indian Gallery and the Naval Gallery were destroyed together with the whole of the tropical department with all the lofty palms, the rare and lovely plants and flowers. The Colossal Egyptian figures also perished together with the orangery, the reading-room, the School of Art and the Queen's retiring-room. A chimpanzee, a baby hippopotamus and many birds were killed. It took two years to rebuild the north wing but owing to lack of money the north transept was never replaced.

It would be wearisome to describe, or even list, the succession of events which followed each other over the years. They culminated in the 'Festival of Empire' held in 1911, the year of King George V's Coronation. For this occasion the British Empire was constructed in miniature in the Palace grounds, complete with three-quarter-size replicas of the Parliament buildings of all the Commonwealth countries. These replicas, their exteriors architecturally complete to the smallest detail, were built of timber and plaster. Exhibitions of the products of the appropriate country were on view inside.

On a miniature railway, aptly named the 'All Red Route', visitors could tour the Empire and stop off, amongst other places, at a South African diamond-mine, an Indian tea plantation and a Canadian logging camp. This was the biggest show ever put on at the Palace and although it attracted hundreds of thousands of visitors from all over the world it did not save the Crystal Palace Company from bankruptcy that same year. An order was made to sell the entire property, then valued at a mere £230,000, and it was bought by the then Lord Plymouth who wanted to save it for the people.

A Lord Mayor's Fund was then set up to raise the money to relieve Lord Plymouth of his responsibility and in 1913 the Palace became the property of the Nation. By that time the building, starved for so long of proper care and attention, was in a very poor state and it deteriorated further during the First World War through being used as a naval depot. When, in 1920, it was reopened to the public the Palace was near derelict and the task of restoration facing the Trustees was a prodigious one. They were fortunate in their choice of a managing director for Sir Henry Buckland was a man of unusual ability and energy. Under his guidance the Trustees repaired and overhauled the building, cleaned and rearranged the contents and set the inside fountains going once more. The gardens were cleaned up and replanted, the terraces weeded. The constant job of painting the fabric of the Palace was restarted and the visitors began to return. During Sir Henry Buckland's

Right 'Festival of Empire', 1911. Some of the Commonwealth buildings and the Sou African diamond-mine.

Below right Opening Concert for the 'Festival of Empire'.

1. Australian vineyard.

2. South African diamond-mine.

3. Indian tea plantation.

4. Newfoundland building.

5. South African building.

6. Maxim's flying machine.   *Right* Bird's-eye view.

7. The Topsy-Turvy.   *Below right* The Canadian building.

1

2

3

4

5

6

JOY WHEELS & MAXIM FLYING MACHINE.

7

THE TOPSY-TURVY, CRYSTAL PALACE

administration, a yearly revenue of £80,000 was built up and on this relatively small sum he saved the building, kept it in reasonable condition and built up a reserve fund.

On some afternoons during the school summer holidays, and always on a Thursday so as not to miss the fireworks, a schoolfriend and I used to visit the Crystal Palace, arriving early in the morning and leaving when it closed at about 10 p.m. For the best part of the day we usually had the entire forty-four million cubic feet to ourselves for the firework crowd did not arrive until the evening. My memory of the place is dim but enduring. I remember the echo of our footsteps and voices in the great emptiness of the nave. I remember Osler's Crystal Fountain and the row upon row of busts of artists and musicians, poets and dramatists, kings and queens, scientists and writers, soldiers and statesmen, all neatly lined up in classified and chronological order like a Madame Tussaud's in plaster. I remember the seemingly interminable tiers of the empty Grand Orchestra, climbing up to the Great Organ which, so far above us, appeared not great at all. And I also remember the naked stone ladies whose expressions of indifference or coyness seemed feigned through the biological embellishments that had been added to

their bodies by generations of small boys. The 'nude male statues' of the 1854 controversy were also there still, their plaster fig leaves mostly chipped or broken away, to reveal a lack that seemed far more obscene than the presence of 'the parts which in life ought to be concealed'. The souvenir stalls had gone long ago and the bars and refreshment-rooms were always closed. In the gardens the fountains had dried up and some of the statues and urns had been overturned but the Great Maze was still there as were the artificial caves and the stone monsters.

The terraces, lawns, flower temples and shrubberies were a little shabby but crowning them still was the translucent mass that was the Crystal Palace and in the rays of the sun it was a mountain of light. I never tired of the place.

xtreme left The Palace grounds were a
ourite haunt for courting couples. Its 200
res of woods and shrubberies with their
aries, temples, terraces and shelters
re ideal for romantic dalliance.

ft One of the stone monsters by the great
e.

ght The Imperial War Museum found
nporary rest from its wanderings in the
th wing.

low Part of the nave as the writer
members it. Vast and deserted, dusty and
ittle dreary. Yet it never failed to
vide a whole day's entertainment and
usement.

Below left The south transept and the nave ablaze.

Below right Collapse of the southern half of the nave.

Bottom The south transept minutes before its collapse.

Previous pages The Crystal Palace, 30th November 1936. The question that puzzled the thousands of spectators was, 'How can iron and glass burn so fiercely?'

11
THE END

'A blazing arch of lucid glass
Leaps like a fountain from the grass'
(THACKERAY)

At six o'clock on the evening of 30th November 1936, Sir Henry Buckland, on his way to post a letter, noticed a red glow within the central transept of the Palace. On investigating he found one of the resident firemen and some workmen trying to put out a small fire that had broken out in a staff lavatory. The only other people in the building at the time were a group of musicians rehearsing in the Concert-room and Sir Henry sent a man to tell them that there was no danger. The rehearsal continued but a few minutes later the man hurried back to advise the musicians to run for their lives. Within five minutes of their departure the Concert-room itself was ablaze. The line of the Palace ran from north-north-east to south-south-west and the wind was blowing from the north-west. The fire, which had started in the front of the main transept, crept out of the lavatory and with frightening speed swept to the back, down the nave and into the south-west wing. The dry wood of the gallery floorboards, the walls and the sashes burnt like tinder and within half an hour the building was an inferno from end to end.

As the flames spread the wind grew stronger, fanning the fire to even fiercer intensity. Whole squares of glass were blown high into the air to dash down in the surrounding streets. By the time the Penge Fire Brigade arrived the whole of the central transept which contained the enormous wooden orchestra was alight and they could do nothing to check the fire's spread. From all over London fire brigades arrived bringing with them 89 engines and 381 firemen – nearly half London's total strength. With them came the crowds of sightseers and an army of foot and mounted police. I was at that time living four miles from the Palace and although far too young to be allowed out alone after dark, I made my way as if mesmerised towards that ever-increasing glow of fire in the sky which I had first seen from a window of my home. Hundreds of others accompanied me through the suburban streets that climb towards Sydenham Hill while thousands more stood at their front gates wondering on, or openly disbelieving, the news that iron and glass could burn so fiercely. My own feeling of absolute incredulity was sadly shattered when I arrived at Crystal Palace Parade. The familiar iron arches were silhouetted against the roaring inferno like the bars of a huge furnace and it was obvious, even to me, that the brass-crested firemen, dwarfed against a back-cloth of flaming fabric, were fighting a losing battle. The stream of people converging on the building was enormous and continued until 2 a.m., thronging the Parade and the surrounding streets, trampling down fences and front gardens.

Many fire-engine crews had to stand by helplessly until mounted police were able to force back the crowds and barricade the streets. Only then could the turntables and water-pumps be operated, but even these were unavailing. It was as though the thousands of tons of water that were hurled against the blaze had no effect at all. Section by section the great iron skeleton, white-hot in places, collapsed in showers of sparks and bursts of flame which at times reached a height of 300 feet. The collapse of the Great Transept was heard 5 miles away like the thunder of distant cannon. No one of the generations of Brocks could have conceived of such a display of fire even in their wildest dreams. Shortly before midnight the fire reached the south wing and from there it leaped across to the south tower. But before it gained a strong hold the main building had been consumed and the firemen were able to concentrate their efforts on saving the tower, the collapse of which would have spelt disaster to the surrounding property. A little after midnight only the towers and the red-hot framework of the north wing remained. Colonel Sibthorpe would have danced with joy.

The great fire had been seen by thousands who had gathered on every prominence in London, and private aeroplanes from near-by Croydon Aerodrome crossed and recrossed the bright red sky. The fire was even visible at Brighton. Hampstead Heath and Blackheath were still crowded at 2 a.m. for even then the great area of red-hot iron, molten glass and smouldering wood was casting its red glow into the London sky.

Sir Henry Buckland had watched the disaster from beginning to end and when at last the flames died down he spoke to the reporters with tears running from his eyes.

On the morning of 1st December all that remained of the building once described as 'a symbol of universal happiness and brotherhood of mystical significance' was a gaunt framework and

Sir Henry Buckland regarding the end of his twenty-five years' work.

All that remained on the morning of 1st December.

a few smoke-blackened statues standing on the terraces, fearfully contemplating the still smouldering wreckage and, in the north wing, some bronze nymphs gazing mournfully into an ornamental fountain, where, incredibly, there still swam some goldfish. *The Times* reported them as 'missing, believed boiled'. The nation was bitterly grieved by the loss of one of London's famous and favourite sights and *The Times* summed up this sadness in a leader on the disaster which ended '*Simul omnes collacrimabunt*, for its burning down is a real calamity.'

The Palace and its contents were insured at Lloyd's through a 'first loss' policy for £110,000 and exactly one week later Lloyd's paid this pathetic sum in final settlement. The Great Organ was separately insured for £10,000. Sir Henry Buckland received thousands of letters of sympathy from all over the world and two weeks later *The Times* was still printing readers' letters about the tragedy. One, referring to the Palace as 'a monumental relic of the golden age', asked, 'Are we sure that the Crystal Palace cannot be rebuilt? – The cost would be less than that of a battleship.' Another reader wrote of the 'loved and lamented Mecca of all good Englishmen and women', and still another, 'We were at the height of our glory in 1851 – where are we today? Let us hope the disappearance of the

The ruins of the north end of the nave.

Left The Assyrian Court.

Centre The Egyptian Court.

Right The Byzantine Court.

Bottom left Osler's Crystal Fountain remained upright despite the collapse of the roof.

Bottom right Osler's Crystal Fountain in its heyday.

Palace may not be an omen.'

But omen it was. The sinking of the *Titanic* in 1911 was, we are told, a prophetic symbol of the passing of the Edwardian Age which was to perish with the First World War. The destruction of the Crystal Palace portended the end of the age-old system of values, attitudes and morals already being undermined in the 1930s and which was to be swept away finally by the war of 1939. Amongst the many events cancelled after the Palace burned down was one at which 30,000 schoolchildren were to have heard Miss Gracie Fields sing in honour of the forthcoming Coronation of King Edward VIII. The children would have been disappointed anyway. The constitutional crisis concerning that lovelorn monarch was already front-page news and ten days after the cremation of the Crystal Palace the King abdicated his throne to marry an American divorcée. This was one of a number of events which helped to tear up the remaining roots of the nineteenth century. The war which followed so closely behind brought with it acts of savagery and destruction without parallel in the history of civilization while our heritage of that struggle – the atomic bomb, the rocket and a bitterly divided world – has made the Victorian dream of peace embodied in the Great Exhibition laughable in its naïvety. The eighty-five

years of the Palace's existence were, perhaps, the most significant in the history of Europe. During that comparatively short period, Darwin, Freud and Picasso did their best respectively to destroy the old conceptions of God, the soul and art while, towards the end of it, Hitler and Stalin got well on the way to destroying civilization altogether as Einstein unwittingly worked on a formula for a future generation to use in the incineration of the world. The aims of the Crystal Palace were creative and pacific and, if it had to go, it is fitting that it went when it did.

Brunel's water towers survived into the 1940s like two towers of silence mournfully commemorating the past. One of the excuses given for their demolition was that they acted as a London landmark for enemy bombers. The same reason could have been given for the dynamiting of St Paul's Cathedral. One of them could and should have been left standing as a relic of that unique, historic building and as a monument to the high endeavour of its creators.

The grounds of the Palace, shorn of fountains and temples, are now a public park and all that remains intact of Paxton's enterprise are the prehistoric monsters which still manage to instruct and amuse. Near by the newly erected National Recreation Centre disfigures

left A nymph mourns as the north tower topples.

below and below left 'Forward, forward, let us range, Let the Great World spin forever down the ringing grooves of change.'

top right 'The trumpeters and pipers are silent.'

centre right 'How time is slipping underneath our feet: Unborn TOMORROW and dead YESTERDAY, why fret about them if TODAY be sweet!'

bottom right 'Lo, all the pomp of yesterday is one with Nineveh and Tyre.'

Below **The prehistoric monsters still haunt the park.**

Bottom **The Paxton tunnel, still intact, is to be preserved as an historic monument.**

Right **Sir Joseph Paxton, MP, one-time gardener's boy, still surveys the site of his masterpiece.**

the scenery. This forbidding edifice is in stark contrast to the elegance of its predecessor, being rather more comparable to the 1851 Committee's ill-fated design for an exhibition building. The actual site of the Palace and its terraces is fenced off and reserved for a proposed National Exhibition Centre, the building and aims of which will probably cause both Joseph Paxton and Colonel Sibthorpe to turn in their graves. The visitor can still walk along the foundations of the old building, and if he is of an imaginative as well as a sentimental turn of mind his fancy may still conjure the barking of a multitude of dogs, the rejoicing of a thousand Hallelujah choruses, the sonorous booming of generations of leather-lunged brass bands and the flutter of myriad canaries and pigeons.

Over the foundations looms a television mast which reminds us that while the Crystal Palace slowly waned in popularity John Logie Baird was busy in the south tower inventing television. It is a strange contrast; from the site of the Crystal Palace, dedicated to the recreation of the past, professional iconoclasts now make their aerial contribution to the mass of mind-bending trumpery trash which is the mainstay of twentieth-century entertainment and art.

The remains of the stately terraces are still there, the alcoves, alas, empty; but on the broken balustrades a few plaster figures still face the ravages of time. At the end of what was once the elm-lined Grand Avenue the colossal stone head of Sir Joseph Paxton, one-time gardener's boy, surveys the ruined site of his masterpiece.

APPENDIX 1

The Hyde Park building.

The substratum of the Hyde Park site consists of gravel and this was found to be sufficiently dense to sustain the weight of the building without deep excavations. Concrete pads were laid to take the base plates which were to support the 1074 8-inch columns and, in order to avoid a complete levelling of the site causing damage to the Park, the base plates were set at varying heights to suit existing ground-levels. The columns were hollow castings and in addition to supporting the roof and galleries, they served as pipes carrying storm water from the roof through special connectors at the base into the main drainage system. The tiers of columns were linked together by means of special castings, the meeting faces being lathe-turned to exclude the use of packing pieces. There being no internal dividing walls to brace the structure the squares formed by the columns and transverse girders were strengthened by diagonal rods connecting the top corners. At their intersection in the centre of each square there was a cast-iron ring to which ornamental faces were later fitted.

The first tier of columns and girders supported the galleries, each 24 feet wide and extending through the whole length of the building in four parallel lines, diverted only by the transept, round the ends of which they continued. The galleries were reached by eight double and two single staircases, the treads of which were made from sabicu, a species of very hard mahogany, the risers being of deal. Numerous cross galleries connected each pair of longitudinal galleries.

The uppermost tier of girders supported the roof which, although its general form was flat, was made up of a series of ridges and furrows. The roof girders were arranged at 24-foot centres and laid transversely to the main axis of the building. Spanning between them at 8-foot intervals were light rafters hollowed out on top to form gutters. These special members were called 'Paxton gutters' after their inventor. Intermediate and parallel ridges were formed by the intersection of glazing bars at a gentle slope of 1 in $2\frac{1}{2}$ and rainwater collected in these valleys was conveyed through the Paxton gutters to main transverse gutters above each girder, and thence to the hollow columns. To carry off water formed through condensation on the inner surface of the roof, channels were incorporated in the underside of the Paxton gutters and these, too, discharged into the main gutters.

The glass used throughout the building was one-sixteenth of an inch thick and weighed 1 lb per foot superficial. The standard size of pane was 49 inches by 10 inches and the aggregate weight of glass used totalled some 400 tons.

The transept was formed with four arched ribs of memel timber also placed 24 feet apart. Each rib was made up of three thicknesses of wood, the centre core being 4 inches thick and the outer pieces 2 inches thick. The wood was shaped in 9-foot lengths which were so fastened together as to ensure a staggered joint, i.e. the joints of the outer pieces coincided with the centre-line of the inner core pieces and the whole assembly was then bolted together at approximately 2-foot intervals. Between the ribs there were purlins fixed 9 feet apart with cast-iron shoes. The purlins supported intermediate ribs which were built up of a square section of timber flanked by two thicknesses of 1-inch board specially bent round to form valleys. To these the glazing bars were attached in the same manner as before, the spaces below the first row of purlins being fitted with louvres which could be operated from ground-level. The semicircular ends of the transept were filled in with quasi-Gothic tracery formed by radiating timbers strutted with concentric rings. The semicircular head of each segment and the semicircular eye from which the tracery proceeded were iron castings and the ribs forming the tracery were moulded on the outer face having glazing bars fixed to the inner face. The only parts of the roof which were not transparent were two lead flats on either side of the tran-

sept. These served as working-platform[s] during the operation of hoisting t[he] bonnet-like roof of the transept and al[so] gave additional strength at the springi[ng] of the arched ribs to resist any tenden[cy] they might have to spread outward[s]. Diagonal tie-rods on the inside co[n-] tributed further to the stability of t[he] arches and, in addition, produced [a] agreeable play of lines over the surfa[ce] of the roof. The very simplicity of t[he] construction made it easy to disman[tle] transport and re-erect in a larger [or] smaller form.

Most of the woodwork and a great d[eal] of the metalwork were prefabricated [on] the site. The Paxton gutters were ma[de] by passing wood through a plani[ng] machine, a multiple groove-cutti[ng] machine and an end-finishing machi[ne]. The glazing bars were cut and drilled [by] machine and there were on the site al[so] a mechanical adzer, a mechanical meta[l] puncher and shearer, a power-drill, [a] handrail-cutting machine and a machi[ne] for painting the glazing bars. After da[rk] light for working was provided by lar[ge] bonfires of scrap-wood and shavings, a[nd] on one occasion twelve of these fires we[re] kept burning all night.

APPENDIX 2

Digby Wyatt's description of the raising of the transept roof in Hyde Park.

The operation about which most anxiety had been felt was the hoisting of the arched ribs of the transept. These ribs were constructed on the ground horizontally, and when completed with all their bolts, two of them were reared on end, and maintained in a vertical position, at a distance of 24 feet from each other, by guy-ropes. As the ribs singly possessed little lateral stiffness, they were framed together in pairs with the purlins, intermediate small ribs and diagonal tie-rods, forming a complete bay of the roof 24 feet long; two complete sets of temporary ties were also introduced to provide for the strains incident to the variations in position of the ribs during hoisting. The feet of the ribs were bolted on to a stout piece of timber, and the lower purlins strutted up from the same.

The whole framework was then moved on rollers to the centre of the square formed by the intersection of the transept and the main avenue, where it was afterwards hoisted. All the ribs were landed over this square, and were afterwards moved on a tramway formed of a half baulk of timber constructed over the columns on either side of the transept, at a height of about 4 feet above the lead flat. The hoisting-tackle consisted of four crabs, each one being placed on the side of the transept opposite to the part of the ribs to be lifted by it, so that the men at the crabs might watch the effect of their exertions with greater convenience.

The hoisting-shears were placed on the lead flat immediately over the deep trusses of 72 feet span; each set consisted of three stout scaffold-poles, lashed together at the top, and footed on planks laid across the flat, and secured by the necessary guy-ropes. The hoisting-rope passed from each of the crabs across the transept horizontally, to a leading block attached to the foot of the opposite angle column of the square; it then passed up to a treble block fastened to the shears on the flat, and from thence down to a double block secured by chains to the bottom part of the ribs.

There was a peculiar difficulty to be overcome in this operation, which arose from the circumstance that the width of the framework was greater than that of the transept, the extreme width of the framework to be hoisted being 74 feet, and the clear width apart of the trusses over which it had to be hoisted being only 71 feet 4 inches. It was therefore necessary to raise one side to a height of 35 feet before raising the other, so as to diminish the horizontal width of the whole, the diameter of the semicircle being maintained at this angle: the whole was then hoisted, until the highest end could clear the tramway.

The foot of the ribs on one side was then passed over the tramway sufficiently to allow the other side to clear the opposite truss; after which the whole was hoisted to the full height, and rested on rollers of hardwood placed between the sills attached to the framework and the tramway, by means of which it was moved to its permanent position. There it was again raised by another set of shears, while the sill and tramway were removed from under it; and the ribs were then lowered into the sockets prepared for them, formed by the continuation of the columns above the level of the lead flat.

Every successive pair of ribs was fixed at a distance of 24 feet, or one bay from the preceding one; and the purlins, etc. were fixed in the intervening space without any scaffolding from the ground, by means of jointed ladders, which were adjusted to the form of the roof.

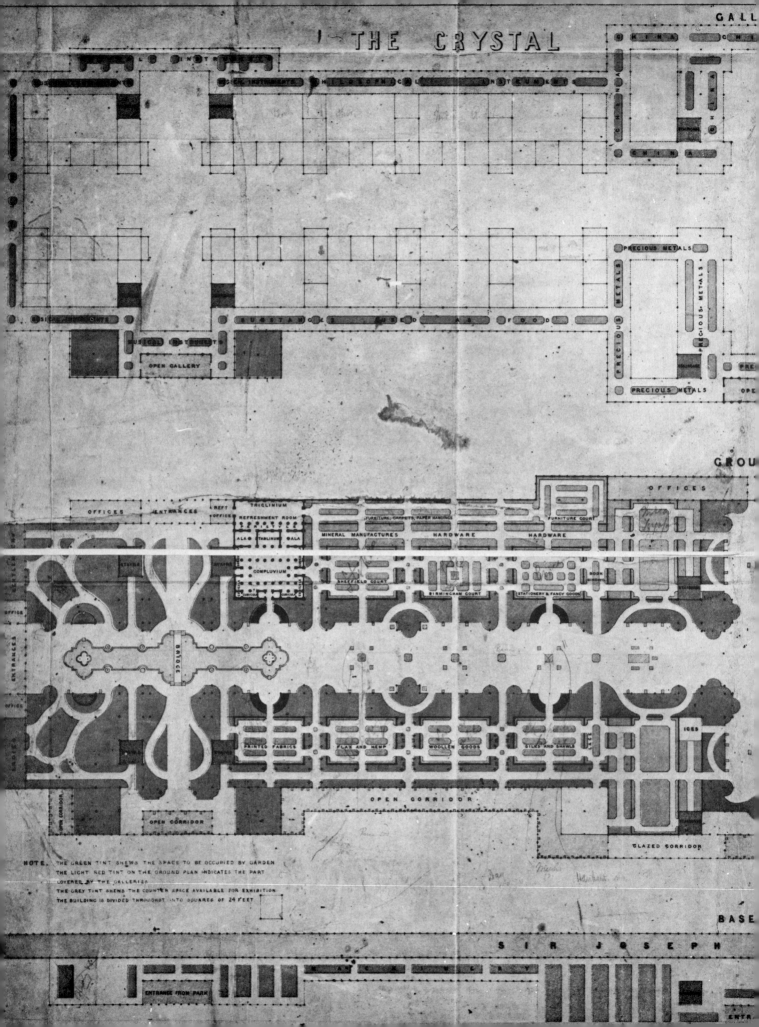

Books are to be returned on
date below.

057056